WAIST

DEEP

IN

BLACK

WATER

John Lane

John

Lane

WAIST

DEEP

IN

BLACK

WATER

The

University

of

Georgia

Press

Athens

and

London

Published by the University of Georgia Press
Athens, Georgia 30602
© 2002 by John Lane
All rights reserved
Designed by Sandra Strother Hudson
Set in Walbaum by Graphic Composition, Inc.,
Athens, Georgia
Printed and bound by Thomson-Shore
The paper in this book meets the guidelines for
permanence and durability of the Committee on
Production Guidelines for Book Longevity of the
Council on Library Resources.

Printed in the United States of America
06 05 04 03 02 C 5 4 3 2 1

Library of Congress Cataloging-in-Publication Data

Lane, John, 1954–
Waist deep in black water / John Lane.
p. cm.
ISBN 0-8203-2461-2 (hardcover : alk. paper)
1. Nature. 2. Lane, John, 1954– —Journeys. I. Title.
QH81 .L23 2002
508—dc21   2002006414

British Library Cataloging-in-Publication Data available

For Betsy

Contents

Author's
Note

Many people helped me along the way with this collection. Many even became characters in the pieces and will now remain so. My debt to each of these companions is literally as obvious as the words on the page. Without our shared experiences I would not have these stories to tell.

I would hope that all included would remember that this is a book of memoir. I wrote each story from memory, recreating the situations from the near and far past as best I could. The personal essays are works of the imagination and I've even, in a few cases, changed names and left out people who contributed much to the journey.

For travel, spiritual support, and adventure I would like to especially thank photographer and friend Mark Olencki, David Romtvedt, Margo Brown, Jeremy Jones and the staff at Sayre School, Michael Branch, David Taylor, Doug Raynor, Gerald Thurmond, Arlene Burns, Thomas Rain Crowe, Nan Watkins, Jim Proctor, Jenny Wooten, Terry Ferguson. Special thanks to Ab Abercrombie for walking the edges with me and helping to pay my way to Florida and Mexico with his grant money and to Kim Phillips for introducing me to Suriname and the meaning of its true wildness.

Judith Kitchen read the full manuscript of "A Stand of Cypress" and made valuable suggestions in its early stages when it looked like I would get a book out of my two weeks in Florida. For help in the later stages of development, when these various pieces finally fused into a collection, I would like to thank Betsy Teter, Beth Ely, Cathy Conner, Susan Tweit, and Deno Trakas.

Dean Maultsby and President Dunlap at Wofford College have both shown encouragement far beyond what should be expected from such a small institution with limited resources. My thanks go to you both for supporting your homegrown poet and essayist.

I would also like to thank the many editors who published these pieces in various magazines. My deep thanks continues to Michael Sternberg, Claudia Brinson, Jennifer Sahn, Betsy Teter, Sean O'Grady, Becky McClanahan, Peter Cooper, Baker Maultsby, Bret Lott, Scott Olson, Dave Smith, Michael Griffith, Judith Kitchen, Mary Paumier Jones, and Barbara Payne and Dale Marie Herring at National Geographic Books. Finally, I would like to thank Barbara Ras, Jon Davies, and the staff at the University of Georgia Press.

WAIST

DEEP

IN

BLACK

WATER

One

EDGES

. . . though we pretend

otherwise, the unknown

increases with the known.

—Wendell Berry,

"The Journey's End"

Medicine
Wheel

The rental contract states clearly that we are not to take the Lumina off the pavement. I read the small print to Mark. If the car breaks down, crashes, or sustains "road damage," all terms of the contract are "null and void." So much for contracts. If we had wanted pavement, we would have headed for Yellowstone. We want gravel and dirt, and Wyoming is known for it. One of the most popular guides for travel in the state is called *8,000 Miles of Dirt.* The Big Horn medicine wheel is at the end of at least four miles of that Wyoming dirt.

This morning we fought our way through an arriving convention of eight thousand Jehovah's Witnesses at the Billings airport, picked up the rental car, drove south, and caught U.S. Highway 14 out of Ranchester, Wyoming, the jumping-off point for an eastern approach to the Big Horns. Highway 14 is blasted into the very stone itself and climbs in every switchback mile through another geologic stratum, moving from the soft sedimentary rock of the Powder River basin's ancient seafloor until it finally peaks out in gray, heavy Precambrian granite.

Rising along a northwest-tending axis in northern Wyoming, the Big Horns are the best-kept mountain secret in the West. Hardly anyone stops, in spite of the experiences to be found in some of the country's highest mountains, deep, jagged, and wild. "The most spiritual people on this planet live in the highest places. So do the most spiritual flowers," the Dalai Lama has speculated. "Life is sparse and sounds travel great distances."

The air is thin at nine thousand feet in the Big Horns, and everything up here, in a geologic sense, seems to me exactly upside down: hard granite, the oldest rock on the planet at nearly 2.5 billion years, should be deep in the earth, not pushed high to the top of these old mountains. But I know deep time and the earth's gigantic convulsions have a way with even matter's hardest expressions. Once before, we flew into Billings, rented a similar car. That time it was Mark's first experience in the big western parks—Glacier, Yellowstone, Teton. The first place he wanted to return to when we planned the second trip out west was the mysterious medicine wheel.

The Big Horn medicine wheel is a place one local tourist commercial describes as "a seventy-foot stone shrine built by a forgotten people in a forgotten time for reasons only they fully understood."

The Forest Service drains some mystery off the wheel with a name: "Medicine Wheel National Historic Landmark." Their small, tan brochure calls the national landmark an altar for "the vision quest" and explains how that quest has always been "at the core" of the Native American religious tradition.

When we stopped on the first trip, we were headed for Buffalo, Wyoming, where we would stay with a friend of mine several days. Buffalo is on the eastern slope of the Big Horns. As we were crossing the mountains, we slid up the dirt road to the medicine wheel because we'd seen the small red cross with the tight print on the Wyoming state map. Mark took a series of photos in our hour-long tourist visit to the wheel. It was those exposures and the black and white prints he made that have drawn us back for a longer stay.

"There's something in those rocks," Mark has said more than once over the past four years. Mostly he has talked about the "faces in the stone," and how he has wanted to get there in the right light and catch them all. I have a hunch Mark is onto something: it is the landscape around the wheel that is drawing us back, not the wheel itself. You could even say we are circling back to work over sacred ground.

Mark is driving. He has a bandanna wrapped around his neck, three days' growth of beard stubble on his face. He's relaxed. The nearest mobile phone cell is a hundred miles away, and Mark's about as far from industrial-commercial photography—how he makes his living—as he can get in the continental United States. And though he misses his wife and little boy, Mark's happy about being out west. I'm happy too. For me, the last semester's English composition papers are finally beginning to recede as surely as the Powder River basin below us.

Our first trip, when we approached from the west, we drove through Yellowstone, Cody, and finally Lovell, where we saw the Medicine Wheel Bar and the Medicine Wheel Motor Court. That's when we looked on the map and spotted the site just off the highway we'd take down into Ranchester. When we crossed the Big Horn River, we could see the mountains rising in the east. The medicine wheel was somewhere between us and the summit of the mountains. There were low clouds like smoke that day, and bikers with rain gear shot past us, headed west, like something out of *Zen and the Art of Motorcycle Maintenance.* I remember the pagan light best of all. Mark made me stop the car, and he tried to catch it spilling out of a dry draw coming off the mountain front. It was as if we had suddenly driven into a fire, the clouds glowing with an eerie otherworldly light.

—

Twenty years ago I started out as a religion major in college. When I was a freshman, I thought I'd end up in seminary at Emory, Duke, or Yale. I was no Bible thumper, though I read it deep and long. I did local missionary work in the poorest junior high through a group called Young Life. My private imagination did not picture "sinners in the hands of an angry God," but my religious beliefs did keep me celibate until my junior year.

I think of this now as my own private glacial age, but I thawed quickly. My third year in college I discovered poetry, Zen Buddhism, and most important of all, the geography of my college girlfriend next to me in a dorm bed. We would spend full, round days there sometimes, naked and alone with each other, a pile of Joni Mitchell records circling on the turntable. Music was our ready sacrament. "I could drink a case of you / and still be on my feet,"

Joni would sing. I tried for two years to drink my girlfriend dry. Somehow in my mind the sweet mysteries of sex didn't go with being a religion major, so I switched to studying literature, spent most of my time the last two years of college reading poetry instead of the New Testament, and wrote short lyrics about having sex with my girlfriend.

Soon after college my poetry left my girlfriend behind (as had I) and centered itself in nature and landscape. I'll turn forty this year, and there is one moraine left from my glacial, religious teens. On churchless Sundays with the *New York Times Book Review,* when it seems for a moment that my spirit and soul can float free of southern Protestant Christianity, I still feel a tinge of guilt for not visiting a place of worship.

It's the return, the regularity of visitation, that I miss, a wheeling childhood certainty. Back then, I knew Sunday morning would mean Saxon Methodist Church. Sometimes I return to an adolescent erection when I hear Joni Mitchell's *Blue,* but sex is not a sacrament to settle my longing for place. Middle age has a way of putting the body in perspective, like looking at a mountain range from a distance and seeing the peaks and the valleys.

Yeats said, "Mankind clothes to ascend, unclothes to descend." Returning to the Big Horns, I am going through a strange reversal, much like the landscape around me. As we drive I take off the clothing of memory—college, my girlfriend, my first poems, the Buddhist monk with the shaved head who once gave me a koan.

Being a sometime Buddhist, I know the present moment is unmistakable. We now have the windows down. We are in the high mountains, three thousand feet higher than anywhere in the East. All around us are purple thistle and mountain aspen, emissaries of those spiritual flowers the Dalai Lama mentions. There is pine smell on the wind as we cruise through a grove of lodgepole pines. It's wild here, in spite of the asphalt highway. Has any religion ever ignored the power of a particular place, especially a place where human beings have lightly passed through, or pass through only briefly? Even Christianity has its wild, windy mountain where Christ retreated before the final test. Relationship to place is a sacrament: geology, topography, weather, plants, animals, light, and memory are terms of our private connection, our contract with it.

—

If Mark has a contract, it is with the changing light. As he drives, Mark keeps an eye on the landscape. Ours is not aimless linear travel. We are on a great circling hunt. We have a destination: the medicine wheel. But the light, Mark's vocation reminds me, always comes before the journey. "This light's from above," he explains out of nowhere. "All the information's straight down."

"Is that good?" I ask.

"If you want to shoot the tops of things, it's good."

Mark doesn't want to shoot the tops of things. So he waits for some angle to develop as the sun declines. We linger at a pull-off. Everything depends on light.

"There's only one rule of light in photography," Mark tells me: "What you see is what you get. You shoot in shadow, you get shadow."

All morning the sky, like the Lumina, hasn't cooperated. There are broken clouds, and then, coming through fast, like huge boxcars of shadow, are the persistent black storm clouds.

"It's like we've been in the eye of something for hours," Mark says, watching the sky. "That storm's been following us since Ranchester." He is leaning on the Lumina's side panel, waiting for the midday light to appear on a house-sized limestone boulder across the valley. He has lowered the window and is talking to me through the opening. All I hear is ". . . waiting for light to bring that to life." His camera is on his hip as he watches clouds and waits for a sheaf of them to slide past the sun. "All we need now is that light." Mark nods toward the limestone, brindled with shadow.

I'm looking through the front windshield at another expanse of limestone. I can barely see two rock climbers on the way up. Their safety rope, bright red, hangs in contrast against the gray stone like thread played out from a spool. One moment the climbers look like tiny ornaments hanging there, and then like Day-Glo lichens. This is the one face the gods show in mountains: *Janua recreation.*

"I am the resurrection, I am the light," Christ sang in a song I had to lead during college on Thursday nights at a meeting with the junior high hoods. Was the light of Christ the same as Mark was waiting for? Back then, I was a Young Life Christian and spent every free afternoon circulating among the hoods, trying to save them from their hormones and hate. I came home every day and collapsed on my small dorm bed, exhausted from my good Christian work. Sex with my girlfriend was a brave new discovery, a place to disappear away from study, family, and work. It was a wickedly dark forest grove. I see now that I was drawn to sex, poetry, and travel in wild mountains for what they shared: each took me to a place free from *shoulds.*

This time, travel has left us sitting on the side of a mountain road, waiting for something as fickle and uncontrollable as the light to change. It is a recreation of sorts. After all, recreation is Latin for "restoration, recovery." The god of this moment is not the god of the Old or New Testament. It is a god more akin to what one philosopher calls "the divine face of things." Sex with my college girlfriend was one of those divine things. Memory still holds on to the innocence of those moments in my college dorm room. I return there when I remember the comfort of those moments across the divide of middle age.

I feel the old comfort once more when I look to the other side of the valley and wait for Mark's picture to reveal itself. Art has taught me to have patience, to tolerate even the waiting involved with someone else's art. It's a sort of grace that Mark understands perfectly. After he snaps three or four exposures of the rock, Mark places his camera carefully like a sacred object on the seat between us through the open window and gets in. Soon he stops again to photograph a mountain aspen grove nearby.

"You're wasting your professional time. Ansel Adams owns those trees," I laugh, thinking of the hundreds of thousands of Sierra Club calendars.

"Adams only leased them for a decade or two. He's dead now. They're back on the market," says Mark.

We're back on the road, and our talk drifts toward the photographers Mark loves. He rambles along the list of his favorites: Weston, always looking under the surface of things; Adams, with his classical themes; Minor White, the philosophical one; and Steiglitz, the promoter.

I tell my favorite photographer story. Paul Caponigro, who spent a decade of his life photographing standing stones in England, Scotland, Ireland, and Brittany, was once at a workshop for photographers, showing slides of his intense, brooding stones. He's a huge man, as large, it seems, as some of the themes and dark stones he has honored with his work.

When the lights came on, one image lingered on the screen, a shot of Stonehenge that would become the cover for Caponigro's New York Graphics Society book *Megaliths*. The first question asked was, "Mr. Caponigro, how did you know to take that picture?" The amateur photographer hoped for some hint at f-stops or exposure or the position of the sun.

Caponigro darkened. "How did I know? It was all quite simple. The hand of God came out of heaven and pointed that way and said, 'There it is, Paul. Don't fuck it up.'"

"Don't you just hate it when that happens?" Mark says. He stops the car. God has pointed his finger, the light tiptoeing over a loaf of granite.

"Up there," I say. "A cairn."

"What's a cairn?"

"Pile of rocks, up there."

Mark looks up the slope, shakes his head, and leans back into the viewfinder, his spiritual eye still wrapped around stones and sky. Moments later he has finished his shot. We hike up the slope and the elevation kicks both our butts. Fatigue is one of the side effects of spiritual pilgrimages to the mountains. The effects of altitude.

Sacred sites have counted on it for hundreds of centuries, and there's no reason to think that the approach to Medicine Mountain will be any different.

Cairns often accompany sacred sites. Most cairns are simply piles of stones with no apparent significance if seen in isolation. They may mark a trail or a significant spot. In Iceland the locals pile them up along roadsides to wish travelers good luck on their journey. There is a famous cairn at the site of Thoreau's cabin on Walden Pond. It consists of thousands of small stones left behind by pilgrims. Many times cairns are positioned in line with one of the four cardinal directions or point toward an important feature in the landscape, such as a stone circle in the Big Horns. If I had a compass, I'd check the orientation on this particular five-foot cairn on top of a green hill the size of a blue whale.

Instead of a compass, I sight off the sun—the yellow disk dropping low in the clear western sky. The cairn is situated in a western line with the medicine wheel. Mark takes a penny out and places it among forty or fifty more in one of the cracks of the piled limestone.

"Offering?" I ask.

"Just lightening the load." Mark takes a few shots of the stack of stones.

—

Ideal male sexuality, like a good cairn, is often seen in terms of vertical staying power, but I see my own libido as a continental ice sheet, receding and advancing as I move from adolescence to old age. Early on, it was the conjugal act (at least imagining it) that made for the great thaw. In old age, I think it will be the warm deathly wind sweeping up from the south.

"'Bout that time to drop that load," a young hood from the junior high would laugh anytime he saw a friend eyeing a pretty girl. Back then, when hormones were just beginning to pool and stream, an erection was the only physical expression worthy of the male body. There were no elegant words, only the beginning of adult physicality and graceful movement. At recess I remember watching young boys, shuffling in herds, hands in their pockets, dumb tongued in the presence of a heartbreakingly beautiful ninth-grade girl. She could probably recount all the parables of Christ and the boy couldn't manage more than a groan. For a young boy, the presence of beauty is a great weight that has pressed up against his vocal cords. "What's your name? Where do you go to school? What do you like to read?" she would ask. He always answered in the language of Neanderthals: a garble, a slurry, pebbles rolling in a raging stream. Only his buddies, hands in pockets, understood.

I did not come to this knowledge easily. It was worn into the landscape of my experience over forty years. Weight as a metaphor for male sexuality never occurred to me until my newly entered middle age, a time when erections diminish and the libido melts away into alluvial drifts and snowmelts, disappearing into the fissures of work and habitual love. Now for me libido bubbles up from the depths as love of place and solitude.

In college, Zen Buddhism seriously eroded my Methodist "do for others" piety. I read Alan Watts, learned to meditate, and even went to a retreat and received a koan, a tiny riddle for me to solve, from a Buddhist monk in from the West Coast. "Who writes," is what the monk offered after two long consultations. I worked on my private koan in my dorm room instead of driving to the junior high to witness to the hoods. I found intellectual comfort in T. S. Eliot's references to Asian religions in "The Waste Land" and ignored his later conversion to the Anglican Church. Pound's cantos dealing with Confucius were revelations, and Yeats's writing in his tower with a samurai sword on his desk was pure jet fuel for my spiritual flights. "Who writes," I repeated, trying to answer it as question, form it as statement. I ended up a college English professor, not a preacher. What else would one with so much on my spiritual plate do? Today, when my students ask me what religion I am, I answer that I'm a Methodist-Buddhist-Pagan.

A confirmed pagan of the moment, I keep the cairn oriented behind me as we drive Highway 14 toward the medicine wheel turnoff. The road circles around the hills, almost doubles back on itself. By the time Mark pulls off at a historical marker in a small park full of boulders, I'm not sure on which hill the cairn is or even if we can still see the spot. A plaque at the pullout is oriented toward the west and explains that the medicine wheel site is still five miles distant. We look west, shading our eyes against the falling sun.

As we drive deeper into the Big Horns, I am looking for a place on which to project the yearnings of my fortieth birthday. I am thinking of it as something of a wailing wall for my lost youth, a memorial for my own innocence. If anything is spiritual for me today, it is movement over wild land and finding my place there.

Looking west from the pull-off, we see the NASA tracking station on Medicine Mountain. "Looks like a big white puffball," Mark says.

"The wheel's just north, on that saddle." I begin to feel it in the distance. First documented in 1895, the wheel is not on most tourists' short list of "must sees" on that summer vacation drive between the East and ragged West. Undeveloped, not easily accessible, the wheel lacks the wonderland geologic convulsions of the Badlands and the hype and history of Yellowstone. Still, if the Forest Service brochure is to be believed, the wheel has a long human history dating back to sometime between 1200 and 1700 A.D.

Most of the wheel's story, as the radio suggested hours earlier, is a mystery. It is this mystery that I find appealing, and I've asked other people why they like to visit the wheel. Mystery keeps coming up. The atmosphere on the ridge in the distance is almost legend among locals in Wyoming. "It's just different," one man says when asked why a pile of stones is interesting enough to bring him up from Greybull once a year. Another woman says that when she visited it the first time, "it was just mist and stones." The Forest Service put up a fence in 1956 to protect the site from people who might move the stones, but many still remember the site in its original austerity.

We drive on. "Look," Mark says, "the wheel's now an official point of interest." On the southwest shoulder of the paved road the sign points off toward a larger sign announcing MEDICINE WHEEL

NATIONAL HISTORIC LANDMARK, which is followed by two or three other signs with information.

On our first trip to the wheel, three years before, there had only been a small green Forest Service sign saying MEDICINE WHEEL and pointing mysteriously up the gravel road. Now Mark turns off the main highway onto a gravel road, and we see the final sign: ROAD CLOSED DUE TO SNOW 2½ miles ahead.

"They've closed off the wheel for solstice," I say, shaking my head. "The native people must have cut a deal with the Forest Service." Native peoples claim solstice as their own. We only see the wheel from a distance through binoculars.

"No, I think they've just closed the road for snow," Mark says. "We'll have to walk in. You can bet they'll have a sign to tell us where to park."

"Snow? It's June."

"It's also nine thousand feet."

"Well, our rental contract doesn't warn us about snow in June."

A mile past the turnoff, the gravel road gets steep, and we strain in lowest gear, and the dust settles behind the Lumina. The puffball NASA observatory looms large on Medicine Mountain, just to our west. There is still plenty of light and the huge blue western sky deepens by the moment—it is a little after five in the afternoon—and we meet two vehicles coming down, one with a Maryland tag, the other a pickup from Wyoming. The driver of the pickup tilts two fingers off the steering wheel; the driver of the car is already lost in the next stop on his tourist map.

We stop the car, see the gate just up the road. Construction. A small settlement is being erected in the wilderness. A cement slab has been laid to the east of the road, and a small dispenser for brochures has been constructed next to the slab. It's the end of the day, and two workers are stretching a dusty tarp over it for the night, as four Forest Service rangers, three men and an older woman, lean on two green trucks and talk. These are the gatekeepers, and this green Forest Service tube locked tight across the gravel road is somehow a threshold.

When we arrived here four years earlier, there was no one waiting to greet us. It was midday. There was no gate. No construction. No rangers interpreting. It occurs to me that we have, without planning, arrived this summer at some vital seam in the development of the medicine wheel, maybe the passage from "site" to "attraction"? Maybe there's finally a need for a gatekeeper, someone to confuse the pilgrims and the tourists. And who better to do it than a Forest Service ranger?

Maybe it's the heat, but the rangers up here look tired, nervous, the way soldiers look at the front. They wave as we get out and gather our gear from the trunk: my backpack, Mark's full camera bag. We stuff light jackets in my pack. I can smell sage. A portable radio the two workers are listening to plays Steely Dan's "Reeling in the Years." They cut the music off and everything goes mountain quiet.

The four sunburned rangers nod as we walk up. They are even more like guardians now, giving up the gate to two late-arriving pilgrims.

Two ignore us and continue to talk. "It's the nicest day I've seen in ten years in the Big Horns," one says to the other.

The woman ranger is the only friendly one. She approaches and tells us they're heading home for the day. She tells us the rules for visiting the wheel: "Stay on the trails, don't take anything or leave anything, and if you encounter native peoples performing ceremonies, please be sensitive."

The workers put their last tools in their pickup, get in, and leave. Then the rangers depart, two in each truck. We watch as their green Forest Service trucks finally disappear down the gravel road away from the medicine wheel. All that's left after the trucks are gone is the harsh sound of the tires on gravel. As they gain some distance, it sounds like distant rolling thunder. Then even that sound disappears, and we're alone at the gate to the medicine wheel.

We hop the Forest Service gate and hike up the trail without song or music, save for the wind. The sun is still high in the western sky. Snow narrows the passage to trail width, fueling the feeling of being in the high mountains. We walk without speaking past the persistent, dirty snowdrifts, the trail dropping off like a Himalayan trekking path on one side, hugging the flank of Medicine Mountain on the other. After ten minutes I finally start an old game we've played for years on trips, mimicking one of our favorite movies, *The Right Stuff*—an exchange between Chuck Yeager and his mechanic before Yeager goes out to meet the demons some say live at Mach One.

"You wouldn't have a stick of Beeman's on you, wouldja?"

"Yeah, I got some right here." Mark smiles, shuffles around film and lenses, finally finds and opens the pack of Beeman's gum.

"Let me have a stick. I'll pay you back if we ever get down to the parking lot again."

Who are the Chuck Yeagers of spiritual Mach One? Who takes the X-1s to the edge of inner space? Since college they have always been the sexual initiates, the mystical-encounter mongers, the LSD and mushroom poppers, the dream junkies, those who pursue experiences not explained by the five senses, or those who push their bodies so far past the five senses they float above fatigue or motor skill, or the artists, those so tuned in to synchronicity that their lives defy rational explanations of circumstances time and time again.

When the snowdrifts finally diminish, Mark zips his camera bag, separates from me, and heads off the trail for the first time. He's spotted some good light up on the flank of Medicine Mountain. Mark wants to get out on the edge of his motor skills, so he begins goat-hopping up along the rim of the Basin of the Five Springs, photographing what he has been talking about for four years, what he saw his first time here, "the faces in the stones."

I break the rangers' rules too, get off the trail, and climb to the razor's edge ridgeline a hundred feet up slope and to my south. I'm walking along the ridge and I'm suddenly in front of the medicine wheel. It's as if it simply appeared before me. It happens that quickly, like one of those spots in the mountains where you pay five dollars to walk into a house that defies gravity. There are four strands of barbed wire surrounding the wheel and each is tied with offerings, "giveaways" as the locals call them. The first time I came here I thought they were to somehow make sure the artifact of the human barrier was in some sort of spiritual harmony with the old wheel, but now, for the first time, I see them as offerings: a film canister filled with wildflowers; a pop-top tied with yarn; a purple pot holder; dangling black beads; a feather bound to a piece of limestone by a string; many shoestrings; a green sock; pinecones; a leather Indian medicine wheel colored red, yellow, black, white; sweet grass; sage; bandanna scraps in red, white, pink, yellow, blue tattered by the wind; a child's shoe; a man's red farm cap; a small Christmas wreath; pieces of dried pine; a small bell tied on a ribbon; an eyeglass holder; a green shirttail flapping in the breeze; a small medicine bundle with mysteries tied inside; a pink hair band; a leather thong; a piece of blue jean, sun faded; a man's white tee shirt. I list these in my journal.

After taking my inventory, I circle once again past the giveaways and the padlocked gate that allows those with a key access to the medicine wheel. It's obvious some people haven't waited for the key, didn't listen to the rangers either. The barbed wire has been twisted until it is slack, and I could squeeze through many spots along the perimeter. But I don't. The fence functions less as a barrier to lawlessness than as a display rack for the giveaways. A friend says that locks function mostly to keep honest people honest. A fence is similar. You can't really keep people out of places they are drawn to.

The first time I made love to my college girlfriend was in the fall of '76, almost twenty years ago. We had the tone arm up on the stereo with the foldout speakers. Joni Mitchell's *Blue* was on the turntable. It was a weeknight, well after midnight. There were papers due. We were breaking college rules, but we weren't about to let a dorm curfew stop the prolonged, lovely drift toward losing our virginity.

I am uncomfortable standing next to the medicine wheel with my hands in my pockets. No woman pushes my heart against my vocal cords right now. Silence is one of the terms of this sacred place, along with falling light, strong memory, and old needs.

Who writes? I do.

The
Once-Again
Wilderness

But I have not only come

to this strangely haunted place

in a short time and too fast.

I have in that move

made an enormous change:

I have departed from my life

as I am used to living it,

and have come

into the wilderness.

—Wendell Berry,

The Unforeseen Wilderness

On an overcast afternoon at the end of October I ride east on I-64 and the Mountain Parkway with a pod of students and faculty in two Suburbans from the Sayre School in downtown Lexington, Kentucky. Mark and I have been invited to come and talk to the students about our collaborations. Though we have worked on place-based projects together in Mexico, Florida, Georgia, and Wyoming, neither one of us knows much about Kentucky, so this is our chance to get our feet on the ground in a new state.

Before we arrived, the teachers had decided we Carolinians needed to see the Red River Gorge, so they set up this photography field trip to coincide with our visit. After a morning of nonstop classes we loaded the school Suburbans and lit out for the territories. The gorge is an hour or so away. The trip is punctuated by the industry of contemporary travel—a lunch stop at Wendy's, on-ramps and exit ramps, and that interstate trance we all know so well. I think of how ancient and undisturbed the word "gorge" sounds next to "interstate" and anticipate the collision of language and landscape to come. Isn't that the transcendental challenge from the nineteenth century, to find a language big enough to fit our landscape?

But we're not all writers in the Suburban. Most have cameras and plan to do at least part of their writing with light. As we ride east into the mountains, I ask Mark, our photographer-in-residence for the moment, about the Kentucky light. "Everything's in the middle today," he says. "It's like we've got a big umbrella over us."

"That's not good," I say, thinking it doesn't sound good. After all, umbrellas might be good for a trip to the beach, but not for trips into a gorge.

"With light like this, shadow can lead us. It's gonna be hard to isolate anything."

I can't imagine anything shadowy in the Kentucky landscape we are passing through—rolling horse pastures and the occasional jutting shelf of bright, cracked sedimentary rock. There seems to be none of the dark density of the granites and gneiss I'm used to in the Carolina piedmont and mountains.

Before we've driven very far east, I'm contradicting myself. I've said I don't know much about Kentucky, but it occurs to me that I have read a dozen books by Wendell Berry and I've met him twice, the last time only a few months before when we were both speakers at a conference in eastern North Carolina. At that conference I was impressed by how aware Berry is of the place he's moving through. I remember, as we headed to the hall for a panel discussion, he walked down the sidewalk confirming the names of the trees we were passing. I look out the windows and hope I can show this land the same courtesy.

We pass a bright blue barn in a field beside the interstate. "Very photogenic," someone laughs at the back of the car. Mark comments that we'd need full sun to make something of that picture, and I think of the struggle to make something out of a landscape with words, the assembling of grammar, syntax, and subject matter into something memorable.

"We are accompanied by the spirit of Wendell Berry," I had commented to the group before we left Sayre's front circle in the two school Suburbans. I explained to them that Wendell has written about where we are going. "Wendell's words have left a trace of himself in the gorge."

Driving from my home in South Carolina, I'd read a section of *The Unforeseen Wilderness: An Essay on the Red River Gorge* to Mark. I wanted us both to know what this most profound of place-based writers had done to make this gorge part of the nation's conversation about landscape.

I don't like to enter a landscape ignorant of its literature. The novelist Walker Percy has commented that writing about place certifies it in a strange way. There's no doubt that a book or an article can anoint a place, give it a capital *P.* I know that Wendell's text and the photographs by Kentucky photographer Ralph Eugene Meatyard have made a difference in people's perceptions of the place to which we are headed. "He saved it," one teacher said when I asked how Wendell's writing about the gorge in the 1970s had mattered.

I'm sure Wendell would call that overstatement. The efforts to stop several dam projects and preserve the unique landscape of the gorge were huge and flooded forth from many fronts. Knowing a place, Wendell has said in his book about the gorge, is "like breathing: it stays real, only on the condition that it continue to happen."

Our trip is happening, and I feel expectant and thankful that we are driving toward a wilderness with twelve students and two teachers instead of answering questions in a seminar, the usual fare on a literary visit. Already I'm looking out the car window, sorting through the hues of autumn trees for the ones I know. There are the yellow poplars and the russet oaks just like back home. There are a few others I know and a few I don't. Looking into the Kentucky woods is like encountering someone in a bus station you think is related, but there's something slightly off. Maybe it's the underlying rock. Maybe it's my own flora deficit.

When I say I don't know Kentucky, what I really mean is that I've never walked the state. I've never touched its rock and smelled rotting fallen timber in its deep woods or waded its streams. The territory is still its map for me. I might as well be looking at an atlas when I move through this country at seventy miles per hour.

When you read a Wendell Berry book—essays, poems, or fiction—you know so much about his place, this place. It's still imagination, though, no matter how you cut it. The imagination, I fear, is not as immediate as walking a stretch of good, hard country that's new to you. Sometimes on afternoons like this I feel I've had a literary lobotomy. Colors and sensations wash over me. I listen to the chatter in the car, mostly about TV shows they watch. "I like the real stuff," one student says. "You know, the Discovery Channel."

Ahead of us I can see billboards for the Tecumseh Wedding Gazebo and the Natural Bridge Cabins. In a moment we will be off the interstate, making this landscape real to us, certifying it.

We climb the ridgeline, slip through the Nada Tunnel, a dream from another time of road building, more horizontal mine shaft than tunnel. I look around in a swirl of amber falling leaves. Below us we see the Wild and Scenic Red River for the first time. There's hardly any flow as it meanders among trees and the first fallen sandstone boulders. The water is gray.

Soon the road narrows and cliffs extend from every ridge. They are like stone birthday cakes someone has buried in the mountains. Someone in the car says this is the "lower gorge." In the woods I can see a tree, exotic and exciting. Its huge copper leaves, vaguely magnolia-like, loll around the base of spindly trunks or hang ponderously from the tips of branches. We pass a pull-off where water bubbles from a hillside and three old men in an ancient, rusted pickup tap bottles at the end of a propped-up pipe. Then we pass a tiny cabin, and Jeremy, the English teacher, calls it a "Unabomber special."

Where Highway 715 crosses the river, we park our Suburbans. This parking lot is where the wilderness begins, 13,300 acres of it, officially named "The Chifty Wilderness." When Wendell came here, it wasn't designated so.

Protection now reigns around us. In 1985 Congress set this tract aside as wilderness, and in 1994 this stretch of the Red River entered the national trust as a Wild and Scenic River.

It's important to note such victories for conservation, but I also note that Wendell tells us in his timeless essay that we are creating the gorge, even as we enter it. We keep it real by our visit.

I am the rear guard as we walk upstream along the river. The cliffs ahead are dangerous. There's a sign that shows a small, dark figure falling from a great height. The photography teacher warns us all to be careful, though we do not plan to climb to the ridge tops along the gorge. We will stay down near the river. Through the trees I can see the sharp bands of sandstone. We're in gorge country, steep grades coming sharply down to the river, and I can see why the 715 bridge divides the country. From here upstream I know that wildness is to be found.

Even with this talk of wildness I search around me for what's familiar. Crow. Kingfisher. Rhododendron, the leaves already curling around the cooling air. Holly. Hemlock. Poison ivy. River birch. The white ghosts of sycamore. There is so much more I don't know. I wander along the path, lost in the wilderness of my own ignorance.

Mark is just ahead of me and he's stopped in a tiny canyon where a small creek runs out from under slabs of sandstone fallen at crosspurposes. They are stacked like abandoned books in a study. Between his feet the river marries the small creek among rounded folds of sandstone.

Mark focuses on the water and clicks off two or three images. Something has caught his eye, something small in this vast, twisting river gorge we are exploring. I look around. There is no perspective here. Too many trees. The people who have lived here were lost in the immediate, all seasons except winter, when things would open up a little. We are down low and the trees shorten every distance. No wonder so many fall from the cliffs. I see a few students

climb to get some perspective, to get, above all, what could be mis-
taken for a stifling shortness of vision.

But I begin to focus on what's around me. Such small things: I
look up into the duff of fallen leaves and see the red seed cluster
of jack-in-the-pulpit and want to show someone. I look closer in
the leaves around me and see the fallen red berries of dogwoods.
"Wasn't all of Kentucky once a shallow sea?" one student asked
another as we unloaded the cars. In the conglomerate rock at the
boot's toe, I see the crescent of a tiny clam pressed into the rock. An
ocean of time at my feet. Plenty of space to get lost.

A wiry man passes me on the trail, headed back from the
gorge. He's shirtless, and tan for October. He's carrying a bundle of
the huge leaves I saw as we drove in. They are the size of beaver
tails and the color of cured tobacco. He holds them bundled in
one hand. He tells me that the leaves are elephant magnolia. He is
a craftsman and he collects them. He'll use them somehow. I tell
him I have never seen anything quite like them in South Carolina. "They're indigenous only to this gorge," he says with pride in
what only his place can grow.

Indigenous. I repeat the word as the pilgrim walks away. What
is indigenous? Certainly not me. But these things are: bright red,
fruiting body of jack-in-the-pulpit high on a sandstone slope.
Bracken fern. Christmas fern. The soft soundscape of crickets. And
now, jet sounds, even here. Would Wendell have heard that?

In *The Unforeseen Wilderness*, Wendell writes over and over
about cycles. His language is Biblical. He talks of vision, of worlds
without end. Once he was in the gorge and it was fall. The leaves
had covered everything, just like now, and he had lost his map. "The
place as it was is gone," he wrote, "and we are gone as we were. . . .
Rejoice that it is dead."

Now it is fall again, and I rejoice that the Sayre School Suburban
has brought me here and dropped me off in the wilderness, fallen
like a leaf among so much beauty. I look up and I'm drawn toward
one of the numerous huge rock shelters in the cliffs above. I remember what Mark said earlier, "With light like this, shadow can

lead us." The shelter opens onto light and then gives way to darkness deepening. I clamber up the scree slope and stand in the entrance. The ceiling is burnt black. From my perch in the shelter, I can see students in twos and threes talking and some sitting along on a rock writing, taking a picture.

I could look around for the map Wendell lost in the wilderness, rotted now by two decades of wet winters and dry summers. I realize there is no need to find it. The Red River wilderness envelops me, its paths and unforeseen places. I take out my journal and note the smell of many fires and the crisp bite of carbon in the air.

Like us, the ancient people came here for warmth and conversation. The gorge opens upstream and down. Below me I can see Mark working the wilderness for the secrets it will divulge to the magic of silver and light. He's still photographing that tiny canyon and creek. I sit for five minutes on my haunches. Mark doesn't move. He's both visitor and local, caught in his aboriginal happiness.

Ascent

and

Summit

"Much of the litter on top of Mount Everest is human corpses," someone reminded the audience on a recent panel at the Community and the Environment Conference in Reno, Nevada. Since returning from the conference I've been thinking about the work of composing a long poem as a kind of Everest experience for poets who choose (or are chosen) to write one. The comparisons are easy. Long poems are time consuming. Because of the commitment they demand, long poems are emotionally, even physically, draining. On the ascent of a high peak there are untold dangers to be anticipated— mistakes and surprises at best; madness, vanity, hubris at worst— but the greatest danger of all may be the predisposition to ascend.

The Reno conference is a unique gathering, exploring, as its brochure explains, "ecological literacy, pedagogy of place, advocacy vs. neutrality, eco-tourism & travel, bioregionalism, land rights and law, community and self." It's the kind of conference I'm drawn to now, the thick-aired life of a small college English professor often in need of enrichment with the perspectives of earth scientists, activists, and ecological historians. It's usually the "community and self" sessions that pull me in. How do we devise ways to rope ourselves together and still retain some sense of individuality?

My flight was screwed up at the back end of my visit to Reno, so on Sunday I took a walk in the hills. I headed into the hills above the university, walking with a friend's dog right after lunch to try to quiet the intellectual demons in my head. I parked my friend's pickup and escaped up a trickling muddy draw, my eyes set on the near-distance where the highest of the hills began to give way to the higher western mountains behind. I thought that if I climbed steadily for several hours, I could make it to the snowy tops of the hills and have a good rest and take the long view. It was a righteous goal.

About halfway up I was giving out in the altitude, so I began to move laterally, traversing a steep ridge spotted with melting snow and loose scree. My destination had become a fist of dark gray stones, an outcrop maybe three hundred yards along the sloping ridge. It was not a dramatic place, but I was drawn there anyway. I could get out of the wind and sit for a few minutes. All the way up I was thinking about ideas that had been circling at the conference. Much of the talk had been of what resides in the land. Was there anything there?

At the conference I had heard an anthropologist talk about his work with the Western Apache. His work with Apache place names makes a convincing case for the connection between Native American place names and the land itself. In it he explores the ties between place, history, morals, manners, and wisdom among these Native American people. Climbing toward the dark stones, I was trying to decide whether this Nevada place had any wisdom for a Southern boy, and if so, what was it?

Soon I came to believe it was foothills wisdom, not summit wisdom. It was muddy, midwinter melt wisdom, a place intent on making me work to find good footing. I had found myself in a place where moving sideways is a happy alternative to ascending. My friend's dog seemed happy with my change of direction, so we continued the traverse.

As I came closer and closer to the stone outcrop, I noticed there was a hawk perched on one of the fingers of stone. It was a large hawk, gray as the backdrop of rock. I moved to my left, gaining a little elevation on the bird with every ten steps or so. It saw me right away but seemed intent to watch me watch it. I worked slowly at first, pausing several times just to watch. The wind caught a couple of feathers and lifted them. The hawk turned its head toward me. As I worked closer, the hawk disappeared and reappeared into the stone, its color and the light such that the sensation was like one of those pictures where if you glance one way the image appears, another and it disappears. Soon I found myself much closer than I expected to be, as little as ten yards away, and the bird had not flown. I thought, "If I ever return here, this Nevada spot will be 'Hawk-Sits-Longer-Than-I-Anticipated.'"

One more step, a little more elevation, three or four minutes of silent watching, and the bird finally lifted into the wind and dropped quickly down the slope. And yet here was the surprise: a second bird, unseen by me until then, was close behind it. They were a pair.

I looked around in the rocks—no nest, but it was obviously a favorite perch for the birds, with the rock stained white with their droppings. What I did then was sit down in a hollow where the wind couldn't curl and contemplated Reno spread below me. I could see the casinos below and the university across the interstate from all the gambling. The dog sat down too, looking out at the view, but not before she had eaten a little marmot shit piled in the crevices around us.

Most poets spend their lives day hiking, attempting achievable summits. But what of the ambitious ascent? "The charge of madness is the common property of poets," writes Guy Davenport on Ezra Pound, "deserved and undeserved." Every time I solve the boulder problems of the lyric poem, I quickly cast my eyes upward toward the madness of the long poem where so many have planted their flag.

Homer, Virgil, and Dante climbed the peak of the long poem, followed in this century by Pound's *The Cantos,* Eliot's *The Wasteland,* and Williams's *Patterson;* even crystal sharp imagist H. D. headed upward, following an icy route to the summit of her long poem, *Helen in Egypt.*

Gary Snyder makes much of ascent and summit in his forty-years-in-the-making poem *Mountains and River without End.* Snyder's 152-page poem moves fluently around geology, anthropology, storytelling, imagism, and the high country of Buddhism and ecology. His poem is a celebration of, to use ecophilosopher David Abrams's phrase, "the more-than-human world." His voice is strong. His purpose is sanity as stated in the poem's opening lines:

> Clearing the mind and sliding in
>> to that created space,
> a web of waters streaming over rocks,
> air misty but not raining,
>> seeing this land from a boat on a lake
>> or a broad slow river,
>> coasting by.

Snyder's time in the mountains lends, it seems, humility and clarity to his vision. This from the section in *Mountains and Rivers without End* called "The Mountain Spirit":

> Plane after plane of desert ridges
> darkening eastward into blue-black haze.
>
> A voice says
>
> "You had a bit of fame once in the city
> for poems of mountains,
>> here it's real."

Snyder's approach to summits, to mountain spirits, has been to leave the ego in base camp. "All the junk that goes with being human / drops away," he writes in "Piute Creek" from his first book, *Rip Rap, and Cold Mountain Poems,* published in 1959. I admire Snyder's sanity. He always has the right shoes, the cleanest route into the high country.

The summer I wrote my long poem, I was probably the closest I've ever been to madness. I was too young (twenty-five); I was broke, unemployed, and lonely; I was reading too much Ezra Pound. But in retrospect (the view from forty-eight), it was one of the few stretches of my life that remains clean of footprints from other projects, other passions.

Pound is renowned for his youthful ambition; he left the United States when he was twenty-two (from Crawford, Illinois, to Venice), and when he finally settled in London, one of the first people he looked up was Henry James, an ambitious social call for an unknown poet. By mid-December 1915 (when Pound was thirty) he had already drafted the first three cantos of his life project, what would be a poem 803 pages in length. Maybe Pound's poem is Everest, and all poets stare upward at its broad back.

Snyder had been thinking about Ezra Pound since college and was already thinking about his long poem *Mountains and Rivers without End* in 1956. He was only twenty-six when he mentioned the idea of the poem to Jack Kerouac on a hike around Mount Tamalpais. Snyder knew he wanted to write a long poem with mountains in it, like the ones on old Chinese scrolls that "merge with the fog in the upper silk void." He already had that vision of the summit. He had written another long poem earlier, *Myths and Texts*, and had become interested in "the challenge of interweaving physical life and inward realms."

The summer of 1980 I was rich in inwardness, but my physical life was in danger. I was so poor I stood in the middle of the downtown mall in Charlottesville and sold my used skillsaw for food money. That transaction was the threshold event. Soon I piled the desk high with books—Pound's *The Cantos,* Hugh Kenner's *The Poetry of Ezra Pound,* Gary Snyder's *Myths and Texts* and *Six Sections of Mountains and Rivers without End.*

By mid-June I was so uncertain whether my meager ration of cash would hold that I flirted with the homely half-wit cashier at the old university cafeteria so that I could slip past with stolen rolls and wrapped squares of butter in my pockets after purchasing a bowl of soup and a glass of sweetened iced tea. "Dollar twenty-seven," she babbled day after day as the summer deepened and the poem lengthened.

My notebooks tell me I was too obsessed with Pound (an anachronism for 1980; an absurdity today). My theme was the self as connected to the landscape I'd grown up with, the Southern Piedmont. I would begin my long poem with a prologue, a catalogue of the natural wonders of the unspoiled Piedmont, precontact, the way Pound had begun *The Cantos* with the tenth book of *The Odyssey*. My long poem began:

From high spine of uplifted rock breaking down
Grain by grain, the erosion of years of sunlight, water
Grinding mountains, the old Appalachian range
To hills and hills and hills

"From this a single human history begins," is how I ended this prologue.

What I wanted was to write a poem rich in the Blue Ridge Mountains and the low places, the swamps and what are called draws in the South, the peaks and vales.

James Hillman says that clambering up peaks is the "search of spirit or it is the drive of the spirit in search of itself." And to drop into the vale? "A depressed emotional place" like (Hillman points out) Keats's "Vale of soul making," or "the vale of tears." Hillman quotes the fourteenth Dalai Lama of Tibet to make his distinction clear between peaks and vales, summits and valleys: "People need to climb the mountain not simply because it is there but because the soulful divinity needs to be mated with the spirit."

In my long poem the countertheme was suffering past the alcoholic mother and the suicide father; my subordinate theme was (yes, I admit to the ambition), "Am I good enough to write the Big One?"

Where did this ambition come from? I think I was channeling Ezra Pound that summer. Old Ez, the spirit of the cold, literary high country, his presence hovering over every draft, every fragment. I still hear his scratchy Caedman L.P. voice in the cadence of my lines, see his New Directions *Selected Poems* clarity in my images; I haunted *The Cantos* that summer looking for an underlying structure; he haunted my poem, demanding ambition.

By late July I had burned out a dozen cheap bulbs in my desk lamp working on my tiny green Olivetti to put all my personal pain and sorrow into stair-stepping lines I'd borrowed from Pound; I honed images to the density of Snyder and Pound. I wrote of remembered wildflowers and the glint of gneiss in a Piedmont riverbed; I howled at my mother for her drunkenness. The long poem—as Galway Kinnell had demanded of all poetry—would contain everything, like an emotional compost heap, husks and rinds simmering and collapsing from day to day in the heat of my composting. By August I had collapsed too. I didn't bathe. I didn't socialize. I worked on the long poem.

Into Thin Air is how Jon Krakauer describes the ill-fated commercial assault on Mount Everest. By late August I was thin as an exposed granite ridge. I had been consumed by my long poem; it was filling out, fattening on my energy. All the sections were drafted. I had nothing else to sell. The air was cooling. My roommates were ready to throw me out for unpaid rent, and soon the furnace would belch into service.

In early September something finally snapped. My notebooks tell me that by midmonth I was no longer writing the long poem. A job? A girl? Somehow recording the means of recovery wasn't as compelling as tracking the possession. Anyway, one summer day I was starving for the long poem, and the next day, as fall settled, the long poem was tucked away in a recycled envelope.

Now the long view from my forties tells me I did not take a wrong route. I climbed and survived. The poem was never published, so for literary history I report that I never really reached the summit. I recall that summer now with the support of a healthy nostalgia, what the essayist Franklin Burroughs calls "partial amnesia and partial denial."

Maybe the long poem will come out of the drawer someday, and

I'll add a fresh snowfield of images and experience to what was laid down almost twenty years ago. Snyder waited years, working steadily on his masterpiece for four decades, never abandoning his work in the lowlands for a permanent base camp high in the mountains. Kitkitdizze, Snyder's home for thirty years in the northern Sierra Nevada, sits at a very livable three thousand feet.

Any artist can understand how I wanted to feel it, that extreme exposure, that clear view of hunger, pain, and poverty, and even that ego free fall into what may have been madness, vanity, hubris. What waited at the end of the climb? If I had continued beyond three months, I would have abandoned all contact with my life, begun to write economic tracts on the gold standard, or maybe won my place among the frozen corpses on some literary Everest. I would not have ended up in Reno, where for me, the "Hawk-Sits-Longer-Than-I-Anticipated." I'm roped in now for the long traverse.

Natural

Edges

Once I lived on Cumberland Island, on the eastern margin of the continent, at a place of merging forms. It was a water land. The sea and marsh drew in around me with each tide, fell away as the tide receded. Live there long enough, Nate, one of the island people, would say, and I'd feel my own being—mostly water anyway— slosh from ear to ear at the pull of a full moon.

I felt the moon pull me often, late at night, away from a book or a letter I was writing and up the trail to leave me sitting for hours watching the water slip up and back. I learned much on these nights, mostly the math of connection: the common denominators among us all. To live on an island is to walk daily on that common ground, to walk the edges of many things.

A dead deer was my first denominator. Curled under live oaks, feet crossed under its body, it was ten feet from the barn where I wrote and slept. It was a big buck, but each day a little more disappeared as the island recycled its own. I watched it decay for a month in the island heat. The body collapsed inward. The carcass supported a congress of insects. Red ants, beetles, flies, wasps, and mosquitoes came and went, working day and night to carry off what they could, bickering and buzzing over the rest. One day the skull was empty. Ants moved out and over the desolate eye ridges.

At night, when the wind shifted east off the marsh, I could catch a strong smell, thick and sweet, a reminder of how close to the edges I lived. It was a mixed smell, but if I worked my nose, I could parcel out the matted green stench of the rotting racks of spartina, hanging salt mist, the dead deer mixed with the marsh and salt, and the drier breezes off the mainland. I was beginning to see that the edge of life is death, or birth, depending on which end of the cycle I wanted to focus. Both were all around me. The world was building the house of birth and death; I lived within it the way I live within my body. All around me the work was going on.

One day I focused on the falling apart, the slowing down, death in all its island colors and states. I walked for hours in the maritime forest, stepping around clusters of dwarf palmettos and over logs and branches. There was no shortage of company; I followed a pileated woodpecker half the distance to the sea, about a half mile, and never lost the hive of mosquitoes circling my head.

There was no loneliness in the woods. I sensed a certain kinship, even with the mosquitoes and ticks; to travel so far and persistently at only the hope of warm attachment is an act not uncommon to my tribe. The air hummed with the hope of sweet conjunction as I fanned away the mosquitoes. To learn to love these creatures was a long mile on the road to heaven.

As I walked, I picked up bones in the woods. Deer, turkey, horse. Even a box turtle's shell. As life scaled my boots and buzzed in my ear, the signs of death were everywhere. I walked and counted out to myself the long list of the dead and dying: dead deer, tree limb, logs, dead wasp suspended by one small strand in a slanting light, a fern broken by strong wind (the wind itself now gone to nothing), a horsehair rubbed against a pine, a standing oak gone to beetles, bones at the base of an osprey's perch, fish skulls, fish ribs. But soon I had walked out of the forest to the first dunes where the forest smells ceased and the air took on the salt smell of the sea.

Another margin. The dune slipped grain by grain into the oak woods, pushing the dunes inward, inland, taking the barrier island three feet eastward every ten years. Suddenly, in the darkness of the oaks, the dunes were a white shock, a running range of sand, a white, head-high wall. I squatted and tried to find the spot where the woods ended and the dunes began, where sand lodges and tumbles among rotting leaves, and leaves rest, half buried, among sand.

When I thought I'd found the place where the dunes became forest, the forest became dunes. I realized my discovery wouldn't last long. The wind stirred, and the edges shifted as new sand settled in the woods. One day I put my finger on the edge of woods. "Here," I said, and planted a twig. The next day I walked back to find the edge. The twig was gone from the spot. I dug a little and found it, not gone, but collapsed under a wash of sand, a small dune. The twig marked a new margin. I felt a strange assurance. I followed twin crescents of a deer trail over the rising dunes into the light outside the oaks.

Two

FIELD

It seemed to him that
something, he didn't know
what, was beginning; had
already begun. It was like the
last act on a set stage. It was
the beginning of the end of
something, he didn't know
what except he would not
grieve. He would be humble
and proud that he had been
found worthy to be a part of it
too or even just to see it too.
—William Faulkner,
"The Bear"

A Stand
of Cypress

Surely one may as
profitably be soaked in
the juices of a swamp for
one day as pick his way
dry-shod over sand.

—Henry David Thoreau

The map of the ranch Smyth had given us looked like one of those old charts followed by the early navigators. There was even a monster guarding the outer boundaries of Anderson Ranch. Smyth's monster was an alligator instead of a dragon, the beast's tail curled over its back, and a puff of wind coming from the toothy reptilian mouth. On Smyth's map there was plenty of *terra incognita* as well; the outline of Telegraph Swamp, the largest privately owned cypress swamp in Florida (owned by Smyth's in-laws, the Andersons), looked like a huge hand with a thick palm, stubby black fingers, and a delicate wrist and forearm pointed south toward Florida's Caloosahatchee River.

I was on Anderson Ranch because my friend Ab had called to ask if I'd be willing to go on a dangerous mission to the Sudan. "If we go, there's a chance we won't make it back alive," he added in his understated way. Ab had been a teacher of mine during my undergraduate days at Wofford College, and I knew he'd been to war, had nearly crashed a Cessna, and had once been bitten by a sidewinder rattler in the Arizona desert, so I had come to understand that the possibility of death determines much of the adventure factor for him.

Maybe we would end up in the Sudan, I thought to myself when

I got the call. Death, be damned. I pulled out my atlas, tried to remember where I'd put my passport. I looked up the Sudan on an African map and traced the blue line of the Nile through rich green ink marshes called the Sudd. There were crocodiles in the Sudd that needed surveying. Somebody had to do it, Ab had said, and there was a possibility, if the government grant money came through, that somebody would be us. I prepared to take my shots and die a heroic research assistant.

As often happens with wildlife schemes, by spring the Sudan had been postponed, the promise of grant money disappearing like seasonal ponds, but another possibility, this Anderson Ranch alligator survey in south Florida, soon took its place.

"We're going into this two weeks of research with about the same resources a biologist in a developing country would have. We've got free lodging in a ranch cottage, a few hours of fixed-wing flying time for surveys, and all the gas we need for the Dodge pickup," Ab explained as we drove down from the Carolinas in late May.

The ranch cottage where we were staying was set back in the pines. It had a bedroom and a kitchen, a TV, even a phone. When we arrived we tossed our sleeping bags on the sheeted beds. Smyth showed us around and then invited us for drinks just before dark, "up in the big house," the Anderson family hunting lodge, then he left.

"Smyth's got an alligator scheme," Ab said as the Land Cruiser disappeared down the sand road. "Maybe we'll hear about it tonight when we go over there."

Smyth's Toyota Land Cruiser was garaged next to a row of personal cars for the visiting Andersons: an antique Cadillac, a vintage Jaguar, and a paneled Ford station wagon. Two green Jeeps equipped with portable deer stands were parked nearby under an old live oak.

The lodge, sided with Anderson Ranch cypress, was nearly hidden within the thick border of the deep swamp. Along the land-

scaped front of the lodge a sprinkler system misted ferns and camellias. This was my first glimpse of the huge swamp, and it was
imposing—like the forests in fairy tales—deep, dark, and silent.
Before we approached the house, I stopped for a moment and
looked toward "the heart of darkness," as Ab was already calling
the stand of cypress. It helped the mood that it was already near
sunset.

We knocked. Smyth answered the door and invited us inside.
The lodge was a taxidermist's dream: a mounted otter, a bobcat, a
turkey, a huge eastern diamondback rattler, and two whitetail deer
heads. Smyth led us to the deck, which jutted over a deep alligator
hole. Ten feet below us cruised several very big gators, obviously fed
a time or two on chicken legs or leftover tenderloin. Across the open
water, as we settled into three flaking metal porch chairs padded
with faded pillows, a limpkin with an apple snail headed toward
the deeper cypress border.

Smyth offered each of us a beer. I accepted. Ab opted for a tall
glass of ice water. Though distant at first, Smyth quickly became
friendly and generous. He explained how he spent one week a
month down on the ranch, managing the financial affairs of the
operation. The rest of the month was spent in the northeastern
home office of his father-in-law. He talked at length about his love
for wildlife and told us that Eliot Porter had photographed along
the edge of the swamp.

"Eliot Porter," Ab said. "You must be proud of that. Not many
ranches have Eliot Porter taking pictures on them."

"My background was in engineering, with ten years of industry
work, but I spent five years consulting for a nature conservancy
group," Smyth said, aware of Ab's tiny jab.

Smyth explained how he even founded a Sierra Club chapter in
a large eastern state—but the future of conservation, he assured us,
as if to establish his position up front, "lies in the private sector."

An obvious believer in free-enterprise—what's now become
known as "free-market environmentalism"—Smyth was most
bothered by regulations, and he ranted against them for a few

minutes as he sipped his beer. In his years in the conservancy group Smyth had seen many "great projects" bogged down in regulations and government paperwork, a problem the private rancher faces as well. The government, Smyth explained to his captive audience, was responsible for the current price crisis with beef. Ab nodded, even though he knew we were part of the paperwork.

Ab followed up on the cattle business, mentioning a recent move by dairy farmers to sell their cows on the beef market, lowering prices drastically. After a swig of Saint Pauli Girl, Smyth joked that he'd "like to grind up my cattle and feed them to the alligators."

"It's a bad time for a cattle rancher in Florida or Wyoming or anywhere else," he went on to explain. "But gator meat is five dollars a pound," Smyth said with a nod toward Ab. "A viable egg is worth twenty dollars. Cows are twenty-three cents a pound to me. That's pretty cheap feed for alligators," Smyth smiled, took another swallow of beer, and shook his head.

Ab was right: Smyth had high hopes for the wild alligators of Anderson Ranch; he had revealed his scheme, but he wasn't saying much more about the details. That would come later. Instead he talked about conservation, as if he had to convince us he was one of us.

Smyth knew we were outsiders in his rich world and only adjuncts to the privilege by way of a government-agency contract. Even our clothes gave us away. We didn't wear the casual golf shirts and expensive hiking boots Smyth sported or the green twill uniforms of the Freshwater Fish and Game people. I was dressed that evening in a tee shirt, shorts, and old basketball shoes. Ab was dressed as always: old jungle boots, a camouflaged shirt with several pens in the breast pocket, and a billed cap, which among southerners is always called a "Cat" hat. The emblem on Ab's hat, one I had brought back for him from Wyoming earlier in the year, said KING ROPES. The words were spelled out with two tiny, continuous loops of rope.

Ab's small web belt was fastened with a simple gold buckle, one of three things Ab had managed to bring back from his tour of duty in Vietnam. (The other two were a canteen and a pair of boots.) On his right hip hung a small, green case where he kept a folded knife and a space pen. Listening quietly in the old, white porch chair, Ab looked more like a redneck deer hunter down from his tree stand than a tropical biologist.

"You could make a fortune selling those bromeliads back in South Carolina," Ab finally said, nodding toward a cypress on the edge of the water hole covered with air plants. Smyth smiled. I could tell that he loved the swamp, loved to be here for a week every month, but he also had an eye for what he called, with no sense of irony, "resource exploitation."

As I sat out the remainder of the evening and listened to Smyth and Ab feeling each other out, I felt like a reporter, not a poet, determined not to put my feelings into words, but instead to catch the scene, the gesture that would fix the reality of the complex surface of Anderson Ranch. I had never encountered a piece of land so large before; Anderson Ranch was a huge piece of Florida, but it was also a huge piece of the issue called conservation. I was beginning to realize that the future of "wildness" on the planet was contained in ninety thousand acres. I had become a player in a larger game for the moment. Ab had led me in with him.

When I was at the end of my beer, Smyth walked us into the edge of the swamp, which sat right in the middle of the ranch, and covered almost one-tenth of the land area. The ranch was in the midst of a long, late spring drought, and the swamp held most of the ranch's standing water. The lodge was on the western margin of the swamp, and south from where we stood stretched Ab's "heart of darkness," six thousand acres of cypress. As we walked into the edge of the swamp, a red-bellied woodpecker worked a huge, dead cypress, twenty feet around at its squat base.

The beauty of the swamp was something atavistic. Prehistoric-looking birds like the woodpecker added to the feeling, along with the trees growing in standing water. It's wrong. There should be dry land and water. God separated the land from the water early on, and only the Devil could allow them to coexist. Black has always been the Devil's color, and there is plenty of black in a cypress swamp. Black loam around the edges where the water has evaporated. Black-silver trees, buttressed at the base, tall and fragile as they ascend, like great gray Goya brushstrokes on a canvas of black. There's always darkness behind cypress trees, because swamps are thick, and this one was three miles thick from north to south.

Near the beginning of the twentieth century, most landowners worked to drain south Florida's extensive cypress swamps with equally extensive canals. Somehow Telegraph Swamp had escaped most of the channeling, although Smyth explained that the flow had been impounded at the southern end by a levee. The drought had dropped water levels along the edges of the swamp so severely that where we stood, the black loam, usually underwater, had dried to a dusty crust. The levee was probably all that had kept vast stretches of water standing in the central swamp.

Smyth was obviously proud of the stand of trees, water, and wildlife. The center of it was a mystery to him, although he was a man who had spent some time in the woods in his life. He had fished all over the West. On the ranch he only had time or inclination to walk into the swamp's margins. The swamp was an unknown quantity, even to Smyth, who spent a week each month on the edge of it, and to the old cowboys who worked this place. It had been left unexplored from the time it was partially logged sixty years earlier. Smyth tipped his hand a little as we walked along. He told Ab he was convinced that we would find many alligators at the swamp's center, in deep water he called "the string of pearls."

As we walked the dry edge of the swamp, Smyth told us how the huge ranch was acquired sixty-five years before, and that under his management he was "trying to redeem the company's bad conservation record."

He told us that in the years after the World War I the Anderson brothers would come down to Punta Gorda, on Florida's west coast, to fish. By 1918 the family lumber business had already "cut a swath right through North Carolina, Georgia, and Florida, and they didn't stop until it reached the Gulf." Smyth told us how on one of their fishing trips the Anderson brothers saw miles and miles of native long leaf pine. "Why hasn't anybody cut these trees?" they asked the locals. "You can't even put an ax in this long leaf is why," the locals responded. So the Anderson Brothers bought 100,000 acres of south Florida long leaf and mowed down every tree for two hundred square miles. Most of the timber went to shore up diamond mines in South Africa. After it was all logged, they slowly worked into ranching, but there was a time, during the depression, when Smyth's father-in-law "would have sold the whole place for ten cents an acre."

Now the pines on the ranch were planted slash, and all that was left of the wild land the Anderson Brothers saw from the train was the big swamp and a few isolated trees like the big cypress we finally circled back toward.

"And I'm *glad* they left it," Smyth said, looking up at the dead cypress and woodpecker. Ab nodded. "Tell me the federal government can do a better job of protecting this than we do." Smyth tapped the big, hollow tree.

We walked back to the lodge, and Smyth offered me another beer. I wanted that beer, but Ab needed to get moving, to get out among the alligators.

As we walked past the camellias and antique cars, Ab finally expressed his feelings about Smyth's possible alligator program. I knew Ab was not a high roller in the conservation game. "But let Smyth do it if he thinks he can," Ab smiled, looking up at Orion's belt, just above the cypress. "Let him fail like everyone else in this state who's tried to raise alligators."

Early the next morning we fixed two sandwiches for lunch, unfolded the map, and placed it in the middle of the kitchen table. Ab took out his Buck knife, trailing the point of the blade down the sand road that followed the west side of the swamp, then turning inland on a trail that followed Moccasin Gully. "This is where we'll go in," he said, "right next to Deep Freeze Camp." The little monster alligator at the edge of the map finally made sense, his tail turned up and a puff of wind rolling from his mouth. We were headed as close to *terra incognita* as we could get in the eastern United States, the center of the swamp, a wild, one-mile-square quadrant of bald cypress and water. Smyth defines wild land as anything he doesn't control. I was to find out what my definition was an hour later when we parked the Dodge truck, sat an easterly heading on Ab's compass, and walked out of the twentieth century into the Mesozoic.

Off somewhere to our east, Smyth had marked "the string of pearls" on the map where he hoped we'd find his alligator Shangri-la: the hidden ponds and sloughs where huge reptiles basked in the sun, waiting to be "maximized," ringed only by a mile of cypress, undisturbed by the passing days or centuries.

Our plan was to walk directly to the center of the swamp and then circle back toward the truck when we found the "string of pearls." Ab led the way. The cypress at the edge of the swamp was only five or ten feet tall, probably pond cypress, much smaller than the bald. Saw palmetto grew in clumps through the distance, like houseplants gone mad in the woods. It was like a toy forest, and we walked through it with ease. We stopped and cut thin cypress poles, and Ab explained how they would serve to probe the deeper water when we approached the middle of the swamp. They might help us discover if there were gator caves in Smyth's string of pearls. But there was no need for the poles yet; on the swamp's rim the drought had dropped the water table. The spongy, dried loam under the cypress and palmetto was much like the land that we had encountered when Smyth took us into the edge of the swamp near the hunting lodge. Cypress stands like the swamp on Smyth's land form along depressions in the limestone, and with normal water levels the ground is saturated all the way to the edge of the stand, but with a drought as severe as the one this area was in, the swamp was like an old sponge left to dry on the sink, the moisture concentrated in the center.

As we walked east, the trees grew larger, and blunt cypress knees protruded like vegetable stalagmites from the mat of last year's dead, brown needles. We were finally entering the bald cypress. It was growing a little darker, and looking up, I could see the "dome" forming fifty feet above us. The swamp began to feel like the fairy-tale forests: dark, open, and somber. The mystery was what was missing. There was no wind in the branches, no frog calls or drag-onflies buzzing past.

Finally, we reached the swamp. When my shoe pressed into the needles, I could see that a little water was beginning to pool around my sole. The water deepened quickly, seeping in over the shoe top. Ab explained how in years of severe drought, fires were known to burn all the way to the center of a cypress dome, killing all the trees and even torching the organic soil. Soon we were calf deep, but Ab led us on. In college we had spent so much time in swamps that we developed a system of gauging depth: ankled, kneed, crotched, and finally, to be waist deep in black water was, indeed, to be waisted.

In a half hour we came to a place where the cypress dome sud-denly opened up, and we could see the sky again just over the top of the buttonbush. The thick buttonbush was just beginning to bloom, the flowers like balls bobbing at the end of the long, whorled branches. Buttonbush can withstand flooding, and it was flourish-ing in the deepening water of the swamp. Ab called this place a "light gap" and said he had noticed many of them from the air, fly-ing over the swamp. He explained that if we were to find much wildlife in the cypress swamp, we would find it here, on the edges of the cypress dome, where there was light, and the underbrush could grow thick. Quickly I found out how dense these "light gaps" could be. They were like natural fences between the swamp and the open places. Ab looked for an opening and began to beat his way through the buttonbush with the spindly cypress pole he had cut. This was Ab's guerrilla war, I thought to myself. Not loss of habitat, but finding habitat where no one had been or cared to go. Ab hacked at the thick buttonbush, brushed against saw grass so sharp it cut his clothes, and looked for gaps in the beginnings of stubby, stubborn willow stands. Several times he had to fall forward and climb the thick brush like a ladder to get through. I followed his trail as best I could.

Ab didn't seem afraid, but I had to remember his year in Vietnam, and his thirty years walking through wild land like this all over the world. The risks weren't so great for him. He'd told me that all his time studying crocodilians would not amount to enough drama "to merit the publication of a two-page article" in an adventure magazine. I didn't agree. I began to think about the danger in which I believed was involved by being in that truly wild place. I tried to list my rational fears. If I got lost, the danger was in not knowing where I was or where I was headed. But I had seen the swamp on the map and knew that a web of sand roads surrounded it, and any one of them would take me some place safe. Getting lost would be bad for our schedule, but not a threat to either of our lives. There was not much chance of me drowning either. The water wasn't deep enough, even in the middle of the swamp. Ab had convinced me that alligators, though large and impressive predators, posed little threat unless we happened to step into a gator hole and land on a big one. That's why we'd cut thin cypress poles and carried them with us into the swamp, to feel ahead of us in the open water. He told me the story of one of his closest encounters with an alligator. He was wading chest deep (off our depth scale) in a narrow, weed-choked slough, and ahead of him floated a large alligator. It didn't stand its ground or quickly splash away, as had been his experience before. Instead, it approached, slowly and deliberately, and then sank silently out of sight.

"At the time I was sure I was being attacked," he said. But he quickly added that he could have misinterpreted the situation, and he assured me that he was in no real danger. "I could have simply climbed out of the water into the saw grass."

I'd been following Ab into difficult places for almost twenty years. He seemed a reluctant, though natural, leader. He had been a teacher, a friend, and an advisor, but mostly he simply pointed the way and then went at it with all his strength to beat me to it. But he was getting tired, beating down the buttonbush and willows enough to go forward. I knew I would have to lead sometime.

"You take the point," Ab finally said, stepping back. So I slipped past him into the lead for a while. Finally, he would be following me.

When we saw the snakes, I began to worry about leading. One, two, then three, four, and five cottonmouths basked in the tangled willow branches. I didn't want to be a leader there. I slowed almost to a crawl, watching where I placed my feet and hands in the thick brush. We were surrounded by cottonmouths. I felt like I had entered a dream; if I had to lead, I would be a rock climber, stuck on a cliff, looking for a nub of rock to hold to, afraid that each would crumble away and leave me falling. The sun was hot in the gaps, and the snakes were draped silently over the branches, lolling on matted grass piles, soaking up the heat. When we came too close, the dark, thick bodies would slip off the branches and disappear into the water somewhere near my feet. This I liked even less. At least I could see them if they remained on the branches.

Looking behind me, I could see that Ab was smiling. "Smyth should ranch cottonmouths, not alligators or cows." Finally, in spite of the snakes, I pushed our path ahead. Sloshing through the cool water, my jeans were covered with green duckweed and dead spiders.

The snakes posed the only real danger I could imagine. I had spent full days in the field and seen one cottonmouth, and we'd been in the swamp for two hours and seen thirty. It was the numbers that brought on the real fear. Some of the snakes were small, but many were arm thick, and I knew enough about snakebites to imagine that if one of us were bitten on the leg or arm by the ubiquitous and sometimes hidden cottonmouths, we would be right in the middle of one of the wildest moment of our lives. It was at least a two-hour hike back to the truck through knee-deep water, not even an easy hike without injury. I remember reading a book on venomous reptiles while I was in college. The authors described the effects of cottonmouth venom on rats. The rat scratched and rubbed the bite from the beginning. Then came a period when the animal sat huddled but alert. The bite area oozed bloody fluid and the swelling spread outward from it. Autopsy showed extensive hemorrhage under the swollen area. I asked Ab if I would die from the bite of a large cottonmouth. "Probably not, but you'd wish you had," he said.

Ab is always understated. He has had his share of snakebite experiences. He had been collecting rattlesnakes in Arizona about ten years earlier, and a friend had just caught a young sidewinder. Ab was holding the bag, and the friend dropped the snake in a little too close to his hand. The snake got one fang in as it was spinning past. Ab spent a night in an Arizona hospital with his hand the size of a fielder's glove.

Then the summer we had spent in Belize on the crocodile survey, Ab and three friends were hauling a canoe up the Macal River in western Belize to check for crocodiles in the dry-season pools. They were forty miles from the nearest road and a good day from the nearest hospital. They had stopped for a few minutes to rest when one of them went climbing on some rocks. Suddenly she yelled, "I've just been bitten by a snake." They hurried to the spot and caught the snake, and everyone was stunned. It was a five-foot *fer-de-lance,* or *Bothrops antrox,* the snake responsible for more deaths than any other American reptile. And their friend had indeed been bitten. The heel of her hand was bleeding.

Ab remembers the next few minutes as the four of them waited for some indication of the seriousness of the bite. There was little else they could do but wait, there in one of the wildest little corners of the hemisphere. They did not want to risk antivenin (which they had among their supplies, but which tends to be as dangerous as the bite itself) until they were sure the bite was serious. Within minutes they knew that somehow she had gotten a dry bite. The snake had not injected any venom. It was a warning bite—fairly common among *Bothrops antrox,* they were to find out later—and their friend would live to leave that wild corner of the world.

I was thinking about cottonmouths so intently that I nearly stepped on a large, basking alligator as I broke through a thick stand of buttonbush and willow. It was six feet long. I jumped back five feet or so in fear. I was stopped, staring down at the alligator.

"It doesn't know what in the hell we are," Ab said.

Neither one of us moved. The gator's back was ashy black, motionless as a log in a small scab of sunshine in the middle of the cypress swamp. Atavistic, like carved slabs of basalt, the reptile's legs rested on the matted straw.

I knew Ab expected me to try to catch this gator. My fear dismantled any confidence I'd gathered walking past the snakes. But I wanted to play the game. This wasn't armadillo catching along the interstate. It was a game much more dangerous. At least it felt that way to me.

I'd give it a try. I approached two more feet.

In daylight an alligator's eye close up is not to be forgotten. Their black eyes hold steady as if staring through millions of miles or years.

"It's backed off about as far as it's going to," Ab said, watching me as I approached a little closer. "Try and hand grab it. We need to find out the sex of what animals we see here in the swamp."

I moved a little closer. "You'll be a legend at the Game Commission," Ab taunted. He has a scar on his right hand where one middle-sized female latched onto him late one night. I remember what he had said: "It wasn't the bite that put me down; it was the infection afterward." I thought about this. Did I have to play his games?

One more step, dragging the duckweed behind me.

"It's a respectable size. A big five." I made a lunge toward the gator as it twisted and sloshed toward the deeper water. It was fast, disappearing into the deeper water in only seconds. And then there was silence. It remained unsurveyed, and I remained without legend. Ab shook his head, tapped at the water. If he was keeping score, then the alligator was ahead in his game.

By noon the water had reached our crotches. We found a dry cypress log suspended over the swamp in the heart of the Anderson Ranch "heart of darkness" and sat down to eat our peanut butter sandwiches. Everything looked the same, gray and quiet. The only other time in my life I'd been in a large cypress stand was in Corkscrew Swamp Sanctuary, about fifty miles east of Anderson Ranch. It is a huge stand, twice the size of this one, probably the finest cypress swamp in the world. Originally it was more than twenty miles long and three miles wide, but logging cut it back to half that size. A two-mile boardwalk winds into the heart of Corkscrew, but you always know the planks, hanging five feet above the black water, can get you out. We were counting not on a boardwalk, but on Ab's compass to get us back to his pickup a few hours later. I wanted to sit with my feet in the duckweed and dark water forever, stare up at the cypress trees, and listen. Smyth was right about the center of the swamp. There was mystery here. Epiphytes were blooming in the crooks of branches, swinging in the slight breeze as if they ate only air. The big cypress cast silver shadows on the clear, black water, and overhead, between the limbs, caught in a web of blue, two turkey vultures circled. But the mystery was deeper than any of those surface phenomena. It was the true mystery of place I felt. This was a spot of no "use" to anyone. Even though we had come to the heart and called it "here" with our human presence, there remained something unnamed among the dark water and brittle cypress.

The mystery was in the quiet, deep as the swamp itself. When I mentioned the silence, Ab gave me a straight science explanation, that "closed-canopy cypress" is quiet because it is "basically sterile, supporting life largely by energy import."

"We'd better not say 'sterile' in the final report," I laughed. "Smyth might read it as an excuse to 'harvest' this spot." Ab said that we wouldn't be able to change Smyth, that the only way a place like the swamp would survive in a capitalist economy was for it to have "a value in Smyth's marketplace." It could be a private hunting preserve, as Smyth had suggested, or it would have to figure into the means of production. "What do you think the taxes are on ninety thousand acres?" Ab asked.

I knew there was more than a chance the reflective Smyth would someday cut the stand of cypress he loved and a large piece of Florida mystery would cease to exist. But sitting there, I was beginning to see the beautiful paradox in the fragility of our time in the deep swamp. What separated that place from Big Cypress Preserve or the Everglades National Park was this fleeting, momentary wildness balanced against the possibility that it would cease to exist, becoming profit or loss in some private corporation's tax return. As we had made our own trail and sat where maybe no one had ever sat, we had found a wild and endangered experience in the swamp, something as rare as the Florida panther. Could Smyth or anyone put a value on our morning in the swamp? Why not assign a "nonvalue" to a few places in the world where such experiences could take place?

"So you've decided you want to change the system?" Ab laughed. "Remember those four approaches: drop out, sign up and become a part of the system—like Smyth, revolt, or compromise."

And Ab's choice? He thought for a moment and told me a story from the summer of 1968, when as a young lieutenant in Vietnam, he had been assigned to II Corps, at a firebase on top of a hill that had been shaved bald, with bunkers dug everywhere. The order came down that they were going to CA—combat assault—into a valley about thirty-five kilometers to the east. They would not make the assault until after dark, so Ab had a whole day to worry. He cleaned his rifle half a hundred times and checked over his platoon until they were nervous as black snakes.

Ab said he tried to sleep but couldn't, so he decided to take a walk. He had never been for a walk in the woods in Vietnam. "No rifle, no radio, no eighty-pound rucksack."

He called the OP in front of his position and told them he'd be passing the firebase perimeter. He finally came to the shoulder of a small ridge where a creek wound quietly down a steep slope. He expected the sound of water, but any sound was muffled in the tall silence of the tropical forest. He said the tall trees, like the cypress under which we sat, "blocked the light so that the dimensions were all vertical. I lifted my eyes upward. . . . It was not that darkness I remember, but the light. Small patches of it, filtering down from above. Flitting across the forest floor like things that were alive. I lay down there, and the light and tall, thin tree trunks took my eyes upward. So high, like a living stained-glass window with a million shades of green."

He paused and the silence deepened around us. "I could have stayed in that Vietnamese forest forever," Ab said. "Or died there, but I came back . . . and compromised, became a tropical ecologist."

In a life packed with required academic and scientific clutter, it was those moments of wildness Ab worked for—time "off the fire-base." But like his story from Vietnam, he was unable to stay there. There was always responsibility.

Although I am not a scientist and missed Vietnam by five years, I know that in the swamp I brushed close to understanding. A mosquito lighted on my wet knee. Its wings stopped. The log was very warm with the noon sun directly overhead. "The name of the game is fixing sunlight," Ab had said earlier in the week, describing energy cycles. Maybe there was one more choice that Ab had discovered but left behind in Vietnam. To sit at the center. Drop in. At-one-ment. I would sit a little longer, fixing sunlight.

Ab stood up and headed off to the west, toward other responsibilities, the unanswered questions of biology and Smyth's "string of pearls." He walked slowly, probing the water ahead of him with a stick, in case a gator had dug her hole there. I listened as, in the distance, a red-bellied woodpecker beat a rough, round hole in another Anderson Ranch cypress.

I sat there a few minutes alone until he was out of sight. It was the point of the whole trip for me, being alone with the cypress. This was one of the remaining wild places in the world; it brought out the best in me. I felt introspective and purified, in harmony with all the plants and animals. But it couldn't last. I didn't want to make my way alone back toward Smyth's world. I headed off through the water in search of Ab.

Soon the water deepened to our chests. Like Everest climbers turned back by a storm, we turned around and walked out of the swamp, not in a straight, scientific transect, but in a soft, looping backtrack, finally emerging from the woods only three hundred yards down the sand road from where we had parked the truck. Ab was disappointed we had not found Smyth's "string of pearls." It, like the alligators that floated in the duckweed there, would have to remain unsurveyed. We would not be the ones to go all the way to the center of the stand of cypress.

My Last
Eden

In our hearts we hope
we will never discover
everything. We pray
there will always be a
world like this one at
whose edge I sat in
darkness.

—E. O. Wilson,
The Diversity of Life

Our first full day in the Suriname rain forest we crossed a tea-dark
creek on twisted roots along a winding, rocky trail. We slanted a
kilometer through huge, gray, granite boulders shaped like clams
and flying saucers. The South American rain forest blocked any
view of the three-hundred-meter dome we were approaching. Our
guide, a Maroon tribesman named Benito, led the way. Then suddenly the dome was in front of us. Benito scrambled upward, brac-
ing occasionally with hands and knees, and we followed, ascending
a long buttress of rock on the west end of the Voltzberg Dome.

The sloping granite ridge, the only access to the dome's summit
without a technical vertical ascent of the granite face, was clogged
with roots and tropical vines. Finally, after a mad scramble along
a thin blade of rock, the dome shook free of rain forest and we
emerged three or four hundred feet above the tops of huge trees on
a slick mossy shield of pure, knobby granite that extended up another 150 meters to the summit.

Climbing to the top of the dome, we could see one of South

America's best kept secrets: spackled through the endless rain forest of Suriname, like carbuncles on the hide of a great, green beast, tall granite domes crack and heave in the tropical heat. Only a few of these domes have been climbed. Some of them haven't even been touched or ogled from close-up. There's one inselberg ("isolated mountain," loosely translated from the Dutch, the colonial language) that one local tribe is convinced is heaven. I've no doubt they're right, and nobody's ever been there to prove them wrong. Even the U.S. Defense Mapping Agency says that the mountain we climbed lies within an area where, if you fly, you have passed "the limits of known topography." Don't fly low if you go through there, or if you do, hope you've got a local god as your copilot.

What took me to a country most *Jeopardy* contestants couldn't place was an invitation from KP, a scientist and former student interested in Suriname as her next research destination after extended stints in Panama and Costa Rica.

When KP was an undergraduate, she fell in love—with dolphins. Though she began her college career as a biology major, she became a psychology major early on because the undergraduate biology department was geared toward medicine. Her shift, at Wofford College, was a matter of convenience. When she fell in love with the dolphins, she figured she could work with them somehow through psychology. Somehow it would all work out. It was a bliss she was following, a glimpse out the corner of an undergraduate's eye. She worked a summer as a research assistant in Hawaii with dolphins. She bought a ring she still wears, a silver dolphin.

The graduate schools where dolphin research was the primary emphasis didn't work out. She ended up at the University of Georgia, and the love for dolphins became an ecological research interest in monkeys. She was the first Georgia psychology graduate student in many years to do field research. She chose as the topic for her dissertation the feeding ecology of white-faced capuchins. After six months of fieldwork in Panama at Barro Colorado Island, her research was done.

Twenty years of traveling have shown me that field researchers in the biological and social sciences are the indicator species to watch if you want to know where the true north of wilderness and adventure might next point. I am not a scientist, but I have traveled quite widely with scientists—tagging alligators in the Florida Everglades, crocodiles in Belize and Mexico. Scientists usually have something very specific they are after—data, research, honor, what E. O. Wilson calls "the labyrinths of field biology and ambition." Like a good scientist, I sometimes travel on my instincts. What I want is surprise, delight, and rapture, and a few thousand words to tell people about it.

Suriname offers KP populations of capuchins to track and study in the vast backcountry. Good research sites are rare, and she is the first scientist awarded research permits in Suriname since the local strongman, D. D. Bouterse, put fifteen of his political opponents in a huddle in the courtyard of a Dutch colonial fort, castrated them, and gunned them down to make his feelings clear about the march of democracy and dissenting opinion in that particular corner of South America.

The government is now friendly and is issuing permits for scientific research again; the government wants tourists to come and visit, especially tourists interested in the rain forest. My bet for the moment is that Suriname is the Land That Time Forgot, but not for long; it is like Belize used to be, with a higher percentage of untouched rain forest than any country in the world and a diverse outgoing Creole culture. It's a little hard to get there. There are only two or three flights a week into Paramaribo, the coastal capital, but once on the ground cabs can take you directly into the old Dutch city on the broad, sluggish Suriname river.

Paramaribo has a good local beer (Parbo) and several cheap, clean guesthouses and hotels to use as base camps for an easy flight by chartered small plane into several interior parks like Raleighvallen.

After a brief stay in the capital we departed for the park. The country's roads are nonexistent, so we didn't plan on driving a rented

Land Rover. There are only one thousand inhabitants in Suriname's great, green, roadless wilderness—various Indians (the rumor being maybe even a few groups uncontacted) and seven tribes of Maroons like Benito, known locally as Bush Negroes. Descended from African slaves, the Maroons escaped into the rain forest and fought two hundred years against the Dutch to maintain their freedom. The Maroons, making up 10 percent of Suriname's population, may be the most neglected, extroverted people in the northern hemisphere. They love company; it's just that it's so damn hard to get into the country they call home that they rarely get visitors.

Our destination was up the Coppename River at Foengoe Island and the research station at Raleighvallen Nature Park. The lodge up the river on the island was once a thriving tourist destination in the golden seventies before Bouterse took power in a military coup. Now the old tourist lodge looks like a long-abandoned set from *Apocalypse Now*—buildings burned in the civil war, rotting thatch, a sagging set of dead electric wires, and a generator crusted up as only fifteen years in a rain forest can crust things up. Though things like lodges fall apart, the human elements—guides like Benito, cooks, and a boatman named Petros, who is as good with a dugout canoe as any Olympic white water paddler—still work very well in Raleighvallen Nature Park. There is a sense that you are in the bosom of an indigenous people who know the forest and want to show it to you. This in itself is a rare and endangered feeling in the emerging world today, where most adventure travel spots have seen more than their share of backpack tourists.

Our goal was not to climb the Voltzberg Dome, though; instead, it was to survey a possible research site for KP's work with monkeys. A day or two into our trip we discovered, with the help of Benito, that the park had so much more to offer besides our hike to the top of the dome; we camped in Voltzberg's shadow, followed new trails through the rain forest with Benito as our guide, saw the breeding ground of the rare cock of the rock, dodged several very poisonous snakes, and finally sighted several species of monkeys, including the capuchins KP wanted to study.

We first found monkeys late the afternoon of our first day in the rain forest when we were walking back down the main trail. Benito stopped suddenly and looked around. "Monkey," he whispered.

"Smell it," KP said. "That pungent odor?"

What I smelled was very much like manure. Sweet. Yes, pungent was a good way to describe it.

"Howler monkey smell," KP said, smiling. "Just like in Panama."

That's as close as we came to monkeys the first day in the forest. The rich smell of howler monkey droppings in the trees. We wondered out loud on the way back why we had not seen anything yet. Were the monkeys testing us to see if we were staying longer than the tourists? Was the forest keeping its animals under cover only for those truly dedicated? Our clothes were soaked from hiking. We were hungry. We had not showered in three days. What else could the monkeys want? KP postulated the worst-case scenario. The guerrillas had hunted out the area during the civil war in the 1980s. They had killed all the monkeys in the park for their cook pots, and the place had had never really recovered.

Besides monkeys, we had seen no other mammals—no agoutis, no paca, no capybara, no sign of the rooting of peccary, no cat tracks. So far we had nothing to report from Raleighvallen but a sense of deep isolation and endless vegetable wildness. And yes, ants.

That first day we walked back to camp with a resigned sadness. The forest was beautiful—"lovely, dark, and deep," as Robert Frost had once described a patch of New England woods—but where were the monkeys we were searching for?

It rained all night but then stopped before dawn. Early in the morning the calling of a troop of red howlers nearby awakened us. They sounded like someone trying to jump-start a chainsaw in the back of an empty van.

When we crawled out of the tent, the rain had stopped. I felt confidence that we would see something new, but when we went into the forest, I was totally disoriented.

"Where is the mountain? Where is the river?" I asked out loud over and over as we wandered through the forest. Benito always knew precisely where we were and pointed his machete toward our two landmarks with unceasing accuracy. How did we know he was accurate? Experience. He always brought us back out on the trail, once less than twenty feet from where we had gone into the undergrowth an hour before.

All day as he walked, Benito not only looked for the monkeys but gathered forest materials to make something. He cut a palm, hacked off the top, and carried a slender, ten-foot section of the trunk like a lance. He scanned the canopy and pulled down a certain vine. When we emerged from the forest late that afternoon, we had seen no monkeys, but Benito had the raw materials for some camp project. After we arrived back at camp, I caught up on my notes. KP looked up several fruits we had found, and Benito sat down and began to assemble a spring-loaded fish trap.

In two hours, after he had finished the trap, Benito showed me how it worked, with a long, arcing "spring" holding the little door open on the cone-shaped instrument.

"I make it for you," he says, handing me the trap. "A gift for you."

I was very moved. This was the first indication that Benito had any real interest in us. I thought we were probably still the two "odd Americans." I went to my pack and pulled out an extra Swiss Army knife I had brought for trading and presented it to him. "For you," I said.

"Monkey, monkey," Benito yelled, running back down the Voltzberg Dome trail. We hadn't noticed that he had wandered off just before dinner. We went hauling down the trail, no machetes, no field notebooks. KP had only her field glasses. We stopped about one hundred yards from camp, and there they were. "I think they're howlers," KP said, but no, then she saw a squirrel monkey moving through the trees.

"Oh god, it's my guys!" she said, her voice growing in excitement as two brown capuchins moved through the treetops above us.

I watched as KP followed the troops of monkeys—maybe five

capuchins and a dozen spiders—off the trail and into the forest. She moved through the undergrowth, not in the direct paths Benito had been guiding us on for several days, but in a wandering meander through the rainforest, going wherever the monkeys led her. Benito followed at a distance.

"They haven't even given alarm calls," KP whispered. "They aren't bothered by us at all."

As we looked overhead, we heard what we thought was another monkey and turned and perched at eye level in a tree not fifty feet away was a scarlet macaw, the closest we'd come to one in our days in the rain forest. The huge macaw sat at an odd angle low in a tree and made a noisy clatter. It was as if all the forest had decided to display its splendor for us!

We sat for fifteen minutes on top of a huge rock shelter and watched the monkeys move overhead. One capuchin carried something that looked like a corncob and KP hoped he would drop it. The spider monkeys followed as the larger capuchins moved ahead of them, headed off to wherever they would all roost that evening. We watched them for forty-five more minutes, until all the monkeys had disappeared into the forest to our southwest. As we hooked back up with Benito and walked back to the trail, he said, "It's a monkey day!" We saw the troop three or four more times over the next two weeks. This assured KP that Raleighvallen was indeed a good place for her research.

When we returned from the interior, we ordered anything on the menu without rice and practiced our own style of fluid replacement, drinking Amstel beer with Sprite chasers. On our first night back in Paramaribo we ran into a Dutch biologist who had worked in Raleighvallen in the late 1970s.

We told him of our climb of the Voltzberg, and he told us how when he'd worked at Raleighvallen if he had not seen his study group of monkeys all day, he would climb the dome just before sunset and watch for the monkeys to come back to a recent sleeping tree. He also told us of another encounter, how he had been run up a tree on the trail to the Voltzberg by a marauding herd of white-lipped peccaries.

"Peccaries?" I said. "That's one thing we didn't see."

"You wouldn't," the biologist said. He took a sip of Amstel and told us a fitting story to sum up Suriname. It was a story about a biologist famous for his work with lions in Africa. The biologist visited Suriname in 1975. He had plans to do jaguar research upriver at Raleighvallen.

"The day he arrived, a herd of white-lipped peccaries swam the river onto Foengoe Island, and much to the biologist's horror, the Maroon guides from the reserve village set upon them with machetes, slaughtering many before the panic-driven animals could swim the remaining channel of the river to escape."

The famous biologist left the next day, abandoning plans for his research, in the face of such a savage display from the park guides. "I understand he attempted his research in Mato Grosso with little success," the biologist added. "Suriname is not East Africa," he said, his blue Dutch eyes brightening. "Maybe he didn't know how wild Raleighvallen is."

The
Crocodile

The earth was flat and
four-cornered. . . . The
sky was multitiered. . . .
the flat earth was thought of
as the back of a monstrous
crocodile resting in a pool
filled with water lilies.

—Michael Coe, *The Maya*

Ab's Mexican friend Marcos wanted to survey the huge, isolated International Biosphere Park called Sain Ka'an, a million acres of mangroves and marsh with an unexcavated Mayan city right in the center of it. Marcos wanted to get some idea of the number of crocodiles in the marshes on the east coast of the Yucatan and whether there was more than one species present. "Marcos also wants to catch and measure a large female crocodile," Ab said, finishing a second cheap burrito at a Taco Bell in Spartanburg.

Ab also had some things he wanted to accomplish. He is a good teacher—particularly out of the classroom—and he wanted to take some of his current and former students into the field once again to try out some theories about wildlife research on a shoe-string budget.

There were eight of us Americans on the trip to Mexico. Back then I was still interested in science and fieldwork, but what I really wanted was a journey in the old sense—a stroke of chance, fortune, and luck. Already I was into a story for the story's sake. They say to be careful what you wish, because the gods will grant it. This time they were right.

Mark was with us as well. He counts himself among Ab's friends, but he is not a present or former student. Mark also wanted adventure. He was a new father and needed the break. Being a photographer, he knew in Mexico there would be good light. He was loaded down with two bags of photo gear and had an eye for contrasts.

Herbert was the oldest of the current students. He was an economics major just graduated from Wofford, half-Mexican and half-Irish. We would come to call Herbert "the Admiral" because he was unflappable, always had an endless supply of fresh shirts from a bottomless suitcase, and exhibited a constant sense of bearing. Mark and I would end up in the canoe with Herbert on our Sain Ka'an survey.

On the way down to Sain Ka'an—Mayan for "birth of sky"—Marcos explained how the entire preserve is bounded on the western edge by Mexico Highway 307, the central north-south route along the coast, but on the eastern margin only a sand two track approaches the high-priced fishing outpost of *Club de Paila*—three hundred U.S. dollars a day to go bonefishing in the lagoons within the preserve. Marcos said he knew the owner and we could put in our canoes at their access dock.

We arrived in Sain Ka'an midafternoon. It was off-season and the place was practically deserted. Inside the gates of the compound there were a dozen thatched roof cottages in the palms, a strip of pristine beach, and a driveway lined with eleven Mayan glyphs concreted onto pedestals.

We drove down the beach and set up camp in the palms. We were a few hundred yards north of a small village, and the children came out and watched us pitch our tents and lay out our sleeping bags for that night. Marcos explained that when the biological park was established, provisions were made for the native people to remain and to retain their fishing and hunting rights within the boundaries. "Of course, the expensive fishing club kept theirs as well," he added.

As we set up camp, Marcos explained the plan for the evening: we would put all our crocodile hunting gear in the Boston whaler and then lash the canoe in the boat.

"Most of us will be in my boat surveying the huge mangrove marsh just off this main beach, but there's a long, natural canal improved a thousand years ago by the Mayans to have sea access from their inland city. We'll drop John, Herbert, and Mark and the canoe at the mouth of that canal at sunset. There's a little temple at the mouth with a tree growing from the top of it. It was a guardhouse or something. I use it to mark my location if I'm on that side of the park. You'll float down the canal and meet back up with us about midnight. We want you to check for crocodiles, and we'd really like to catch a big one, so if you have a chance, go for it."

The *Club de Paila* dock was covered with two well-woven thatched roofs lashed with yellow and black nylon chord, and ten small, fiberglass skiffs with outboards were tied alongside. There were two yellow, high-watt bulbs hanging from coarse wiring. The lights would come into play later, though I didn't know it at the time.

Marcos warned us of storms on the lagoon, as we motored across to the old Clorox bottle that marked the mouth of the ancient canal. "I have seen storms blow up very fast. It is like a sea out here," he said, but the sky was clear that night and no one listened closely. It was too hot, and we were intent on the mangroves in the distance.

Sain Ka'an covers a vast expanse of marsh, coastline, lagoon, and Yucatan tropical forest, the size and in many ways, the texture of the Everglades. Over three-quarters of the park is wetlands, most of it perfect for two species of crocodilians, *C. actus* and *C. moroletti*, the American and the morelette crocodiles, big secretive animals who are spotted best at night from a canoe with powerful lights and silence. The whole place was Mayaland more than a millennium ago.

The best way into the heart of the northern end of Sain Ka'an is through the ancient canal Marcos had told us about. The canal connects the two lagoons and the extensive wetlands. It's a drainage ghost of the Pleistocene and a gift from the Mayans, meandering through the black mangroves and marsh for fifteen twisting kilometers. The natural channel, the result of drainage patterns set up eons ago, was definitely "improved" by the Mayans. As we crept into the narrow channel, we noticed the sides had been squared off and the bottom was very regular. Like an ancient Erie Canal, the canal was used as a trade and travel route for hundreds of years.

Soon after we left the thick coastal mangroves, the canal became as clear as an aquarium. Tropical fish fought the steady current like trout in a mountain stream as the canal dropped the few feet in elevation from one lagoon to another.

As we motored up the canal, Marcos sat on the outboard, swinging and bouncing the powerboat into the thick mangroves like a bumper car. He navigated the short turns excavated just long enough for a Mayan trading canoe loaded down with wood and salt. In the light from a headlamp we saw a bittern, beautifully marked, nesting very low in a mangrove, her one chick standing beside her; she never took flight, just extended her neck as bitterns often do.

Marcos's boat was fiberglass, from which flakes of institutional green paint were peeling. The boat was twenty feet long, piled high with the Grumman canoe and nine people. We grounded out the motor in the bottom sand as the canal became shallow in places. I thought of the meaning of the word "canal"—a watery path between two points—and then, with that definition in mind, I thought of the birth canal and wondered what was to be born in me that evening.

Our destination was the large lagoon to our west and the small ruin of a Mayan outpost Marcos had told us about, which marked the canal's end. The ruin came upon us quickly in the mangroves, guarded by the narrowest stretch of the canal and overhung by mangrove areal roots and a jungle-like thickness.

"There's the ruin," Marcos said, swinging the boat around in front of the small "temple." On first glance at the temple I was reminded of English topographical artist Frederick Catherwood's nineteenth century drawings of the ruined cities of the tropical civilization.

Before us we could see a square, almost boxy stone structure isolated on a built-up spot of a wet grassy plain that bordered the larger lagoon stretching north and south from the canal's mouth. There was one big tree growing from the top (which was also covered with lower bushes and shrubs). As we idled in the canal, Marcos described how archaeologists had cut the roots of the tree in an attempt to kill it, to prevent the ever-expanding roots from destroying the structure.

The crew dropped the three of us at the head of the canal next to the small ruin. We unloaded the Grumman and the gear we would need for what we thought would be a four-hour paddle back to the lagoon east of us and our beach camp beyond: pole and noose for any crocodile over three feet, tongs and mesh bag in case we caught some small ones, paddles, a canteen of water, insect repellent, and two oranges and a lone Snickers bar, in case hunger overtook us. It was still an hour before sunset, Marcos explained, and we were to wait there, near the ruin, until dark, then start downstream through the winding canal.

Soon Marcos started his engine, and his boat pulled away. Ab yelled, "Be careful, and wait for us at the end of the canal," as the boat pulled away.

There was still light, so we climbed out of the canoe to visit the temple. Mark walked around the small dry area of the temple and took photographs. It was a small ruin—two squares on top of each other built out of large squares of limestone. The larger base structure served as a platform for the smaller one, an open room about ten feet above the island. It would have been perfect for a guard tower at the entrance to the canal. For us, it was a starting place, a departure point for our night of adventure. As we circled the temple, we saw it was faced with tic-tac-toe carvings.

"Maybe that's the glyph for crocodile," Mark said.

"Let's call it Xchicklet, 'the small one,'" Herbert said as we circled the temple a final time.

Standing back a little, on the edge of the small spit of dry land, we looked at the lone tree and the archaeologists' so far unsuccessful attempts to kill it. They had not only hacked the roots but also cut the bark away in a band around the trunk; the leaves, however, still seemed healthy, as if the tree were drawing moisture from somewhere besides its roots.

"Looks like they're going to have to do something else to save this temple," Herbert said.

"Save it? This tree has as much right to be here as the temple," I said.

"It's a question of competing agendas," Herbert said. "You want the process, and the archaeologists want the product."

"I like it better with the tree," Mark said, snapping away. "It makes for a better composition."

"See, competing agendas. Once the archaeologists 'discover' it and deem it valuable to science, or to the national heritage, or as a tourist attraction, the tree doesn't stand a chance. People don't want temples with trees on top of them. It isn't natural."

"What will Marcos use to spot the canal from way out in the lagoon if it's gone?" I asked. "It's the highest thing on the horizon."

"He'll get a grant and buy an expensive GPS receiver," Herbert laughed.

We waited for the sun to set over the lagoon. When it was almost dark, I was hit with a huge eruption of Montezuma's revenge. It was the first time in three days. "What am I going to do?" I asked Mark and Herbert.

"Go over there and shit on the island. It's the only dry land," Herbert said, pointing toward the temple.

"Near the temple?"

"Well, you don't have to shit *on* the temple, but you don't have any choice but to shit near it," Herbert said. "You could always hang your butt off the canoe."

As I waited for Montezuma to have his way with me, I thought a little about my predicament. Since arriving in Mexico, I had suffered bouts of intestinal illness. My sickness appeared and disappeared like the sun in the evening, as if it were based on the Mayan concept of time. The Mayans called time the Long Count. All time was circles revolving within larger circles, some with a radius of 54,000 years. Time always returned, but it did not necessarily return with the same content—the same events didn't happen again and again; rather, time returned in a similar form—the same *type* of events happened again and again. To speak in terms of our calendar and not theirs, Tuesday always had its Tuesdayness, and Friday, its Fridayness. The same things might not happen on Friday, but Friday things always happened on Friday.

It is so different to look at time this way, rather than to look at time in our usual linear fashion—what Stephen Jay Gould calls "time's arrow," the idea of Progress, that we set goals in the future and then shoot for them; if we miss the mark, we put another arrow in the bow of the present and let it fly again. Our way of thinking lands men on the moon and finds cures for disease, but it doesn't help us understand a past that won't quite stay past, especially if the past forms itself around the revenge of some ancient Aztec emperor.

I pulled up my pants, buckled my belt, and made my way back to the canoe, where Herbert and Mark were waiting.

"You know that's the last dry land for almost ten miles," Herbert reminded me when I arrived.

"I think I'll make it," I smiled.

The sun was down, and we pushed off into the slight current of the canal. Mark was in the bow of the canoe, and Herbert, like the admiral of some cruise ship, was sitting on two life jackets in the center. He leaned on a thwart, surveying all that we passed.

We entered the mangrove tunnel we'd passed through on the way up, and Mark's Wheatlamp beam filled with insects. He swept the light back and forth over the dark surface of the water. We could see that the canal continued straight and narrow for maybe a hundred yards. We could also see, right away, a crocodile floating along the edge of the canal. Two red eyes shined like rubies forty feet in front of the canoe.

"Good God, there's one already," I whispered. Herbert leaned forward to catch the shine. "And it looks like a big one."

"It must be the guardian for the temple," Mark said.

"Or just one hell of a big crocodile," Herbert added, leaning even more forward.

"Let's go for it," Mark said. "Marcos said he wanted a big one."

"Catch it?" I said, moving the boat forward.

"Yeah, let's catch it. How big do you think it is?"

"Herbert, how far do you think it is between those eyes?"

He leaned even further forward, getting directly behind Mark's light as he kept it fixed on the crocodile.

"Six or seven inches."

"So it's six or seven feet," I said.

"Oh boy," Mark said. "That *is* a big one."

"Well, if you want to try and catch it, get the pole ready. It's now or never. It will be gone soon," I said.

Herbert reached into the floor of the canoe and pulled out the ten-foot pole. It had a wire noose at one end attached to a quarter-inch yellow nylon rope that was duct-taped loosely to the handle in three places. He handed it to Mark, who dropped it low over the water with the noose open, just above the black surface.

"I'm taking you in slowly," I said.

"A little left. It's moving now toward the deeper water," Mark said.

We were fifteen, then ten, then five feet away from the crocodile when Mark said, "Got it!" There was a huge splash and the crocodile headed for the bottom. I heard the duct tape popping on the pole, which Mark passed back to Herbert. "The noose is on, John. What do I do now?" Mark asked, holding onto the nylon rope.

"I don't know," I said. "Just hold tight!"

"What do you mean you don't know?"

"I've never caught a crocodile by myself. Ab's always been with me!"

"Oh shit, it's doing the death roll!" Herbert said, shining his flashlight over the gunnels of the rocking canoe at the crocodile in the clear water below us. Mark played out all the slack, but it kept rolling. "It's rolling up in the rope, doing the death roll, just like in the Tarzan movies!" Herbert narrated.

"Just hold that rope. We've got to get it in the canoe somehow, and we'll get duct tape around its jaws and tie its feet to its back."

"Around its jaws?" Mark asked.

"In the canoe?" Herbert gasped. "Can't we just tow it behind?"

"We got to get it in the boat with us and get it tied up. Get the roll of duct tape."

Herbert looked around. "I think we forgot to bring it."

"What?" Mark asked.

"We don't have any duct tape to wrap its jaws with?" I asked.

"Oh shit," Mark said. "We're near the end of the rope."

Mark wrapped the remaining rope around his hand and began to try to reel in the crocodile.

"It's death rolling the other way!" Herbert said, shining his light at the clear water.

"Here," I said. "There's extra duct tape wrapped around the pole. Peel it off."

I handed Herbert the croc-catching pole and he peeled off a three-foot strip of tape. "This will have to do," I said.

"I'm pulling it up," Mark said, reeling in the rope. "It's coming up pretty easy, like it's tired of death rolling."

The crocodile's head broke the surface between our canoe and the sharp, deep side of the canal. Its mouth was gaping open.

"Let it bite down on that aluminum pole, and we'll try and grab its jaws," I said.

"You try and grab its jaws," Herbert said as he stuck the pole in the crocodile's mouth. It clamped down.

"Mark, can you wrap some of the slack around its jaws?" I asked.

Before Mark could throw the rope around its jaws, the crocodile went down again.

"It's death rolling again!" Herbert said, handling the play-by-play.

After a while it quit rolling and headed back for air, giving Mark some rope to pull up. Soon once again its head broke the surface, the noose pulled tight around its bony neck.

"Okay, let's try it again."

Herbert stuck out the pole for it to grab, and Mark quickly wrapped several loops of rope around the snout.

"Grab its snout. It's secured."

"To hell it is!" Mark said.

"If you've got the jaws, it can't open them. Closing is where all a crocodile's power is. Just grab it and tape it!"

"It's true," Herbert said. "I saw it on *Nova!*"

Mark grabbed and proceeded to wrap the three feet of duct tape around the crocodile's narrow snout. "Okay, it's wrapped."

"Herbert, can you use the extra paddle to pry the croc pole out of its jaws?"

He stuck the paddle in the gap between the crocodile's teeth where it had crunched the pole. Herbert had just enough play to release the pole, but by then the crocodile had clamped down on the plastic paddle blade. "Oh no, now it's got the paddle!" Herbert said.

"Let it have the damn paddle," Mark said. "Cut some rope and wrap its jaws some more."

Herbert cut some rope, and Mark wrapped it around the jaws. When he touched them, the crocodile flipped its head left and let go of the paddle.

"We got the paddle back. Just a few teeth marks, that's all," Mark reported.

"Mark, if we get over and hold onto the mangroves, do you think we can flip her up into the canoe so that we can tie her legs?"

"How do you know it's a she?" Herbert said.

"Just guessing."

"Well, I'll give it a try," Mark said.

"Let's just go ahead and pull her right over into the boat," I said. "She'll give a big shiver if you try."

I still don't know exactly how we got the crocodile in the boat. It took a long time, and it was mostly luck and brute force. Whatever we did wouldn't make it into any technique manuals for handling a crocodile in a mangrove swamp, but after great struggle, the crocodile was finally in the boat with us, tied loosely with forty feet of nylon rope. Herbert moved forward one thwart toward the bow, and we left the crocodile's head at my feet in the stern. It was over six feet and, with its tail curled beside it, took up the good middle portion of the seventeen-foot canoe.

"What are we going to do now?" Herbert said.

"We're taking Marcos his crocodile," Mark said.

"What if we see another one?"

"We'll get close enough to see how big it is," I said. "This is all the catching we're doing tonight."

Was this crocodile the guardian of the temple? I can't say. All I know is how I felt: like we had entered into a great drama. We weren't offstage anymore. We were by ourselves, in the middle of the night, in the middle of an ancient canal, with a crocodile in the boat.

It took us five hours to float down the canal, the crocodile quiet in the bottom of the boat the entire time. The moon was full that night, and by midnight it was up above the southern horizon and the mangroves.

We followed the winding canal without incident. Once we passed a flock of night herons and they took off and flew up through Mark's light and then disappeared in the distance. We didn't talk much. I think at that point we were feeling pretty good, with the crocodile (we thought) secure in the bottom of the canoe. Marcos and Ab would be pleased we had caught such a big one.

Catching a big crocodile had been one of Ab's goals way back at the beginning of the trip, and now it had been achieved. We had made progress. Time's arrow had flown forward. Marcos would have a small bit of needed data, too. The trip had been worthwhile, but that was not enough for me. I wanted to believe that we had been drawn toward the encounter with this crocodile by huge, circling forces. My goal had been to have an adventure, and I had been given it. My adventure was in the bottom of the boat, waiting out the journey. How old was the crocodile? Twenty years? Two thousand? In his last book, *The Demon-Haunted World*, Carl Sagan had cautioned against a retreat into spiritualism and superstition, but you must understand that I was not lessoning the value of the physical world by wishing it to be more than it was. A crocodile is a wondrous thing, and mangroves on the coast of Mexico on a summer night are doubly wondrous. What E. O. Wilson called "the diversity of life," however, was simply not enough for me. My imagination was being pulled toward wider turnings, wider understandings, than what the scientist can impartially observe. "Turning and turning in a widening gyre, / the falcon cannot hear the falconer." wrote Yeats, trying to make sense out of what he saw as a world circling in great revolutions of creation and destruction, much as the Mayans saw the world. If there was a stand to be made at the turn of the century, I'd make it with Yeats. The crocodile would somehow stay crocodile *and* god.

It is safe to observe that we did not see another god or crocodile as we continued to float, but we did finally see the yellow light at the end of the *Club de Paila* dock. We knew we were close to the end of the canal. If we were really quiet, we could hear the surf from the beach as well.

"Almost home," Herbert said when he heard the ocean.

"There's another one," Mark said soon after we'd seen the dock light across the marsh. "It's back in the mangroves. Let's go check it out."

"But we're so close," Herbert said. "I think we should just hang here until the other boat comes back, and then we'll report we saw another one."

"Let's go after it," Mark said. "I think it's another big one. Let's at least get close enough to see how big."

It was all too easy. If this was a true adventure, there had been no real road of trials so far. I knew enough about the "hero's journey" Joseph Campbell had made famous in *The Hero with a Thousand Faces*. I knew there were three parts to every story of adventure—separation, initiation, and return. We had met the threshold guardian, captured it, and carried it along with us. We were about to pass from separation into initiation, the longest of the three stages, where all the true difficulties are encountered. If my hunch about the shape of true adventure proved correct, it was yet to be a long night.

I paddled us out of the channel into the mangroves. It was a deep, long lagoon, with dark mangroves that grew taller the further we followed the crocodile in. "Keep following," Mark said.

"It's leading us away," Herbert said. "Maybe they've set up a crocodile ambush back in the mangroves to get their prisoner back."

Herbert was right. The mangroves behind us looked indistinguishable from the ones in front, and we could no longer hear the ocean or see the light from the dock.

"Shit, we're turned around," I said.

Mark swept the light around the edge of the mangroves in front of us. "It's gone," he said. "We've lost that one."

"And we're lost too," Herbert said.

Just then there was a huge commotion in the middle of the canoe. "It's got the duct tape and rope off its jaws!" Herbert screamed.

The crocodile, free with one giant twist, was loose of its ropes and slipped under my legs and over the gunnel of the canoe into the dark water, still attached by the noose to the yellow rope.

"It's gone," Mark said, looking over the side with his light.

"But it's still got us," Herbert added. "We're tied to it now."

The canoe started to move. "It's pulling us along the bottom," I said. "Look at that." We moved slowly over the surface of the lagoon. After a few pulls, the crocodile stopped pulling and we sat motionless on the dark water.

"We'll wait here for the boat," I said. "We can't be that far from the channel."

"It's 1 A.M. and they were supposed to meet us at midnight," Herbert said. "If they'd have been here when they said they would be here, then we wouldn't be in this fix."

"Well, they're not here and there's nothing we can do about it except wait. And turn your light off. We're getting low on battery power. We'll wait until we hear them before we shine our lights," I said.

We all grew quiet and sat in the dark. We heard the thunder in the distance and saw a huge thunderhead illuminated on the southern horizon.

"What was it Marcos said to watch out for?" Herbert asked.

"Thunderstorms," Mark said with a little disgust, his quotient for adventure well past full. "Looks like we've got one. All we can hope is that it misses us."

We were all in the same boat, so to speak, but we were using different techniques to cope. I had already passed through fear, onto anger, and was in the midst of hunkering down.

"I'm not going to die in this storm," Mark said. "Surely there's something we can do."

"If we'd have planned this all better, it would have never happened," Herbert said.

"Shut up," I said. "There's nothing we can do but wait."

"Let's paddle around," Mark said. "At least we'll be moving. If we die out here, I at least want to be trying not to die."

"We're not going to die," I said.

"You can't guarantee that."

"Look, you two stop arguing," Herbert said. "There are the lights from the other boat."

He was right. There was a weak light like a searchlight on the distant horizon. We could hear the sound of the motor too.

"Turn on your light, Mark," Herbert said. "Yours is the strongest."

"Listen," I said. "Shine your light behind us."

Herbert turned on his light and shined it behind the canoe. The crocodile had surfaced maybe ten feet off the stern. It had its mouth open and it was hissing loudly.

"John, it doesn't like you one bit," Herbert said.

"Why me?" I said. "Mark's the one who caught it."

"Yeah, but you're the one steering this boat," he said.

Then the crocodile disappeared below the surface of the lagoon.

That was the moment when I was most frightened that night. I really believed, though I didn't tell Herbert and Mark, that the crocodile was out to get me, and me alone. I sat in the dark in abject terror while several times the crocodile rose from the darkness, mouth open, and hissed. I knew it would snap its jaws shut on me and drag me into the deepest water, thrashing me side-to-side until I was dead, dismembered, gutted. It is in our fears that the gods extract their greatest revenge, the Greek tragedies tell us.

"Let's go, John," Mark said. "We've got to get to that light."

We paddled toward the boat's light, working our way around one wall of mangroves after another, dragging the crocodile behind us like a sea anchor. At one point we saw the yellow light from the dock and heard the sound of the ocean, but we quickly lost the boat in the heavy mangroves. We'd hear the boat's motor sometimes, and other times we'd see the boat's light, but we didn't really seem to be getting any closer.

"I've fucking had it," Mark said finally, slapping the water with the canoe paddle.

"So what do you want me to do?"

"We shouldn't be in this situation," Mark said. "They should have left either Ab or Marcos with us."

"Ab can get lost too," I said.

"Not like this," Mark said. "We are dangerously lost, and I don't like it one bit."

I didn't answer, kept paddling, and then stopped. The crocodile would surface directly behind me each time we stopped, and my fear would return. It would hiss and disappear into the water again. What was it? Who was it? What god? What fear?

The moon was completely down, and it was dark with the lights off. At one point we sat and held onto the mangroves as the storm passed just to our south. We could smell the rain it was so close. We ate the two oranges, the Snickers bar.

"We're lost, we are deep lost," Herbert said. "We've been out here too many hours."

We discussed how bad it could possibly get as we drank the last of the water in the canteen. I suggested the worst that could happen was that the crocodile could eat one of us, and if that didn't happen, the worst would be that we'd be out all night, and in the morning, we'd find our way to the ocean and walk down the beach. This didn't make Mark feel much better. He was pissed off that we were lost in the first place. "They'll get an airplane," Herbert said cheerfully. "They can find us that way if they have to."

"Let's cut this damn crocodile loose at least," Mark said. "It's slowing us down when we look for an opening."

"We caught it, and we're hanging onto it. It'll die if we cut it loose with that noose around its neck," I said.

"Okay, so we don't cut it loose and we die."

"We're not going to die. Besides, if it eats one of us, it'll obviously choose me," I said, motioning over my shoulder at the hissing crocodile.

I've often thought about that situation. If the crocodile were not simply a crocodile, acting as a crocodile would act in a situation of stress, what was it? I guess I am asking the question science always backs away from: "What did that experience mean?" If that night sitting with two frightened friends in a canoe was an initiation, what was I being initiated into? A brotherhood? A priesthood?

It would be easy to say that our croc capture added a little data to Marcos's study of the crocodiles of Sain Ka'an. That's not enough for me. I like to think the initiation granted me membership in both brotherhoods—with Mark and Herbert—and a priesthood. But priest of what? Not science, that's for sure. The imagination? My own arching life as a writer?

We had been in the canoe nine hours when we saw the light from Marcos's boat coming toward us from around a wall of mangroves. When the boat got close, we could see Ab in the bow, Marcos sitting on the engine.

"How are you?" Ab said.

"Lost," Herbert answered. "Deep lost."

Ab and Marcos reeled in the crocodile and caught it easily, put it in the motorboat.

"It's the biggest croc we've caught in here," Marcos said. "You did a good job. Where did you catch it?"

"Twenty feet downstream from the canal," Mark muttered.

"It was in the canoe with you at one time?"

"Yeah, until it got another notion," I said.

"Congratulations," Ab said as he measured the crocodile with his tape and checked the gender. "You were trailing a six-foot female crocodile."

They led us to the deep water to get both boats out of the mangroves. The tide was out and the water was quite shallow. I had watched the sky all night, just like a Mayan priest, looking for an answer, but one did not come until the ordeal was over. It was almost dawn, and the morning star, Venus, was rising over the ocean. The sky was becoming very blue by the time we reached the dock.

Climbing out of the boat, I had a vision of sorts, of Kukulcan, the earlier Mayan face of the later Aztec god Quetzalcoatl. I knew that Kukulcan and Quetzalcoatl were both associated with Venus, the bright returning planet, and that the myth of the white-faced Quetzalcoatl's return to Mexico from the east made for easy entry into Aztec Mexico of Cortés. Vision or not, what I was really seeing was Venus for the first time.

Marcos told us that they had dropped the others at the dock when the storm approached, but it was too late. The storm had hit our camp, the wind ripping the tent pegs out of the sand and scattering all the tents down the beach. "One of the Mayan woman in the village found a rain fly in her cook house," Marcos said. "It was one big storm. Glad it missed us. It could have been trouble out on the unprotected water."

We arrived back to the dock just as dawn broke and Venus disappeared. I was exhausted. I walked down the path toward where our encampment had been reestablished, and one final strange thing happened. A pig came out of the brush and followed me back to camp, walking at heel like a dog. It was a male pig, a very friendly pig, rooting happily in the sand around the tents. I crawled into my tent and went to sleep. When I woke hours later, the pig was still sitting there, next to my tent. Ab called from the camp stove that breakfast was ready. When I crawled out of the tent, the pig finally wandered away.

Maybe that pig had seen me through to the some new beginning and knew that I needed some help reentering the world. Food is always a good place to start. On that morning in the land the Mayans called birth of sky, I remember I ate fresh eggs with hot sauce, with stacks of tortillas to sop up the broken yellow yolks.

Three

HOME

TERRITORY

Our behavior toward
the land is an eloquent and
detailed expression of our
character.
—Stephanie Mills,
In Service of the Wild

Something Rare as a Dwarf-Flowered Heartleaf

It's a sunny Friday afternoon in mid-March and I've asked Doug, a friend and Wofford College botanist, to show me a local plant on the Federally Endangered Species List, the dwarf-flowered heartleaf *(Hexastylis naniflora)*. It grows at Camp Mary Elizabeth, a Girl Scout camp within the city limits of Spartanburg, only a few minutes drive from the campus where I teach. For weeks now many in the community have been debating whether Camp Mary Elizabeth, a sheltered fifty-six-acre creek draw surrounded by subdivisions and dense commercial traffic, should leave the protection of the Girl Scouts and be developed. I want to see the camp for myself for the first time in years, and I also want to see the dwarf-flowered heartleaf in its native habit, what Doug calls "Piedmont bluffs." Somehow in my mind the two issues are forever linked, the hopeful survival of a rare urban camp with its rustic atmosphere of retreat and the quiet, local existence of this species Doug has said is maybe one of the rarest flowers in this upstate South Carolina county.

The camp's acreage, Doug has explained, has a wide range of flora. When he takes his botany class there, they can easily come up with fifty species, not counting sedges and grasses. "Not bad," he says. Doug has said his classes like going to Camp Mary Elizabeth, this surprising woodland preserve so close to campus. There are some interesting upcountry "exotics" as well, Oconee bell, galax, various rhododendrons, all brought in over the last fifty years to make the hilly Camp Mary Elizabeth property feel more like the mountains.

Mary Elizabeth became a cause of mine back in January when a local newspaper article took everyone by surprise and suggested that there was a potential complex development deal in the works. The executive director of the Girl Scouts was on record that the organization had plans for a "dream camp" with a lake, horseback riding, and modern cabins. "These girls want a place away from town where they can do all sorts of activities," the executive director said in the local newspaper. "Right now they think, 'Camp Mary Elizabeth? That's the place on the way to the mall.'"

Conservationists and friends of the camp began to rally soon after the story appeared. The camp has many alumni, and the idea of houses filling the space once occupied by their childhoods was too much to ignore. The week after the article appeared in the paper, a few of us were prompted to attend a city planning commission meeting. We were told that Camp Mary Elizabeth would be discussed. Indeed, after we were seated at the back of the meeting and checked the minutes, we found in the actions under review a paragraph describing how Mary Elizabeth was included in the long-range development plan for the city. My heart sank when I read in their minutes of "the possibility that the Girl Scout camp along Camelot Drive may be sold in the future." The commission's official position on the camp was that it should be kept from "high density development," but that "a planned unit development" would be desirable, given that some open space would be preserved on the site. No mention was made of preserving the camp as a woodland preserve or park. The planning commission had been pleased to have us in attendance, and we left with the sense that city officials at least were interested in this conversation about land use.

After the planning commission meeting a few of us began to make phone calls and write letters. We discovered that the Girl Scouts were not of one mind on Camp Mary Elizabeth. There seemed to be a vocal group not so certain about the wisdom of selling the old resource. We were assured the board was divided on the issue. We contacted the Palmetto Conservation Foundation, a local board member of the Nature Conservancy, and other conservation and land-trust groups. A month into the process we thought we had found the magic "silver bullet" to stop development of the camp. The deed, on file at the county courthouse, had two restrictions placed on it by the original donors. The first stated that there would always be a Girl Scout camp named Mary Elizabeth; the second, which brought tears to our eyes when it was discovered, stated that Camp Mary Elizabeth could never be sold. If a sale were attempted, the property would revert to the original heirs. Unfortunately, after several days of naive elation, it was discovered that the Spartanburg County Foundation, which holds the deed for the Girl Scouts, had in its possession a quit claim deed (not on file in the courthouse) that made null and void the original restriction about sale. Nothing is easy in local politics, especially when a profit is involved.

Will the Girl Scouts and county foundation sell the camp in the near future? Will they consider other options to development? Until recently, the two groups have kept close counsel, but on the eve of the March board meeting a "Fact Sheet on Camp Mary Elizabeth" was released by the official powers. It read like a rationalization for divestment. We have braced for the worst.

To anyone with an eye for profit, Mary Elizabeth seems an almost irresistible asset: "location, location, location, fifty-six wooded acres, a unique creek through the middle of it, much of the land suitable to build on, within the city limits of Spartanburg, dead center in one of the fastest-growing strips in upstate South Carolina." Estimates of the camp's commercial value (also circulated by rumor) have ranged from two million to five million dollars. "That's a lot of Girl Scout cookies," a friend of mine has noted.

—

I have not been to Mary Elizabeth (as the locals call it) in over a decade, maybe longer, though I am no stranger to that area of town. I spent my late adolescence and teen years on Briarcliff Road, less than a mile from the camp. Though I never visited Mary Elizabeth as a child, I remember being aware of it, secluded in the trees to the south of Ezell Boulevard. A Girl Scout camp in the city limits, so close to downtown! That was enough for me then, the idea of a camp within the city limits. It's an idea more powerful than a city park. A park is a compact with openness, with civility. Parks are picnics and ball fields. A camp is a preserve, a retreat, especially a camp within a city limits. For these reasons alone, Mary Elizabeth is an endangered species, a piece of property fit for protection and respect.

When I first set up the trip with Doug, I wasn't getting a good picture of the topography out there. I had looked at a topo map, but Mary Elizabeth was simply an idea, a green-space dream of mine. I had been attending meetings and writing letters and articles for weeks, but I did not feel close to the physical camp except at the abstract level of "cause." I called my niece, who I knew had spent every summer of her early years going to day camp at Mary Elizabeth. What did she remember? The way, when her mother dropped her off at camp, the city seemed to cease to exist for the day. The sound of water rushing over the stones. "Walking all those trails through the trees," she said, "camp outs, archery, swimming in the swimming pool, wading in the creek. You know, regular camp things."

I needed more connection. I needed some idea of what makes the property unique and valuable beyond real estate. The Girl Scouts' administration seemed willing to abandon fifty years of tradition and memory for the new dream of a place in "the country." What were they leaving behind? What could another group (besides a developer) seize on and utilize about this significant acreage in the midst of a sprawling city? I was hoping it would be this tiny plant, the dwarf-flowered heartleaf, and the woods that surrounded it. I knew it had to be something that local, that specific.

Doug's silver van pulls into the parking lot about three in the afternoon. Another friend is coming along as well. Gerald gets out of his red and white pickup, wearing his signature brown cowboy hat and his hiking boots. "You brought your field glasses," Doug says as we load into the Toyota. "Warblers," Gerald says, smiling. "I'm after warblers."

I've always enjoyed going into the field with those more scientific and observant than I am. People like Doug and Gerald notice so much, miss so little, because they never seem to turn sullen and crawl into their head, jousting with invisible windmill developers and politicians. At least not in my presence. The woods bring them out, focus them on the things outside like bird migrations and blooming flora. They help to pull me out of myself too. I try to horn in on their discussion, already at full tilt, of migrating warblers and what bird songs they've heard this week.

We leave Wofford via West St. John, the 1970s cut-through created to drain the traffic past the dying downtown. Spartanburg's thirty-year-old Bradford pears are in bloom. Planted after the traditional oaks were cut to widen the streets, the pears have fared poorly in this Piedmont city. They are scarred where branches have been ripped off, battered by every passing storm. They are quite beautiful for a moment each year, and then the blossoms turn a sickly dusty gray.

Spartanburg, a Piedmont city thirty miles from the Blue Ridge, is said to have been founded by four men sent into the eighteenth-century wilderness to scout out a site for a courthouse. They tired of their travels, settled under an oak to rest, and drank deeply from a jug of whiskey next to an up-country spring. If I look too closely, it seems as if the city planners and residents have always been drunk with the latest plan to turn around the disaster of a downtown.

Riding through town, I'm thinking how the more I talk to people about Camp Mary Elizabeth, the more I am overwhelmed by how clearly the fate of these fifty-six acres of hardwood on the edge of town is tied to the collapse of the center. Now, after years of neglect and abandoned renewal projects (including a downtown outdoor mall and a huge, incongruous skyscraper built in the 1980s by an overvalued fast-food company), Spartanburg's downtown is said to be recovering. As we drive through, I can still see it's in critical condition, though; huge tracts of what was once a thriving county seat and business district stand idle: empty buildings, vacant lots, an unusable parking garage. These days there is a $122 million renaissance project in the wings to try another jump start with a big hotel and a golf course. I've been told there are those in Spartanburg's political and economic elite who see Mary Elizabeth as a key to continuing the critical recovery. It could be a seed ground for pulling the wealthy back into the city. If we can just develop an upscale housing community there on the west side, surely we can bring back some of those high-dollar senior executives from the suburbs farther out in the county.

We've done the sprawl thing badly in Spartanburg, maybe even worse than most communities that grow fast and furiously. As we drive west and downtown recedes quickly behind us, we pass the ancient ring of strip developments from the fifties and sixties: vacant lots, a dilapidated fast-food restaurant, an abandoned drug factory. The commerce in this zone is now small-time operators looking for cheap rents: used-car lots, Zippy Marts, pawnshops.

Rather than talk about what we are passing through, Gerald and Doug discuss a friend's sighting of a woodcock near his home out in the country. The bird is doing a seasonal mating ritual every morning and evening. They coordinate an early morning meeting as Doug downshifts past a loan company and a Church's Fried Chicken. I continue to watch the cityscape through the big windows of the van. As I look out, I hope for a real renaissance, a cultural, social, or political rebirth. To look closely at the edges of this city is to get depressed in a hurry about the way the finger of New South commerce moved through, leaving its dirty scrawl (quick profit and shabby construction) as its signature.

—

A half mile from downtown, Doug finally has some open road. Where West Main crosses Fairforest Creek, the street turns into divided four-lane, Ezell Boulevard, the road west out of town. In my childhood Ezell Boulevard was a well-kept garden, four lanes with a tree-shaded median strip. Thousands of flowers bloomed in the spring. Many of the city's leaders lived along the boulevard in the fifties, sixties and seventies. W. O. Ezell lived along its course as well and spent thousands of volunteer hours working with the Men's Garden Club to keep the "west gate" of Spartanburg beautiful. Later, the city was so appreciative of Mr. Ezell's work they renamed West Main Street for him. Today, thirty years later, Ezell Boulevard feels neglected as the fifties and sixties upper middle-class homes that line it have fallen on harder times, needing paint, up for sale, growing more vulnerable to creeping strip development from the west.

What has protected Ezell Boulevard from commercial development west of Fairforest Creek is topography. The heavily and deeply down-cut nature of this particular part of the city makes commercial development expensive. Much fill would be required for level ground. The names of local neighborhoods show that this is higher country than the land to the east: Park Hills, Vanderbilt Hills, Woodland Heights. On spots along Ezell Boulevard there are even little waterfalls where tiny streams fall toward the creek. And for me, driving out along Ezell as a child, it was always exciting to look through the thick hardwoods and see the little rivulets tumbling over exposed stone. It felt like the mountains, thirty miles to the west.

Those childhood days saw the four-lane stop at the intersection of I-26 amid old cotton fields and trees. The west of Spartanburg was so empty until the early 1970s that the U.S. Army conducted war games there in 1966, Swift Strike III. These days the area a half mile west of Mary Elizabeth is defined by a square mile of sprawl known as Westgate. At the height of the shopping day the population density of this area probably approaches that of Tokyo.

This junction of Ezell Boulevard and I-26 is economic hell: traffic patterns defy logic; Wal-Mart, Sam's Warehouse, Super K-mart, Home Depot, Lowe's, Circuit City, Best Buy and the Westgate Mall itself spew Suburbans and BMWs into four lanes of traffic headed in all four cardinal directions; square miles of parking lots sweat beads of petroleum into storm drains and creeks; small shrubs and trees struggle for space in vast slabs of asphalt; inside the mall, thousands circulate in a jerky shopping dance, half need, half desire; clerks hawk name brands and scan credit cards; teens hang loose and noisy at electronic arcades; elders read detective novels in the artificial light as the round-leafed rubber plants vibrate to the Muzak.

———

We try Mary Elizabeth's main gate just off Camelot Drive, the 1980s cut-through street between Reidville Road and Ezell Boulevard. The long, pine-filled sweep of Elizabeth frontage has kept what would surely be a subdivision from filling one whole side of the road. The gate, black, imposing, and ornate, is closed and padlocked securely. The local Girl Scouts have since the 1940s kept their headquarters on the camp property and this street side entrance is their driveway. Doug explains how he usually drives in, parks his vehicle, and walks down into the quiet and solitude of Mary Elizabeth.

We had forgotten that in the last couple of months, the Girl Scouts headquarters had been moved to a strip development in the midst of the west side. The executive director did not feel safe deep in the woods of Mary Elizabeth, so she had moved the headquarters. "We wanted a location where everyone could feel secure . . . At night it's real scary here," she had said. "We wanted to increase visibility." At the December board meeting the group approved a ten-year lease from a local developer for office space. The terms of the lease have yet to be disclosed. The developer also agreed to pay for sixty thousand dollars of renovations.

We all agree we should not give up on our field trip so easily. We should go back around to the original 1940s entrance to the camp, just off Ezell Boulevard. Doug knows how to squeeze past the gate and enter the grounds from that direction as well. "This will be interesting," Doug laughs. "Three local college professors arrested."

"It will make great copy," I say. "Three college professors arrested for viewing endangered local plant."

The entrance to the camp is hard to reach. The two brick pillars with plaques (dedicating the camp in 1946 to the memory of Mary Zimmermann Ward and her daughter Elizabeth Ward Cannon) are lodged in a confusing snarl of an old carpet store, roads without street signs, and a half-dozen houses about a hundred yards off the busy boulevard. Even Doug is a little confused. I'm reminded of how difficult it is to sort out the conflicts of interest in this struggle. There is the city, with its hopes of revitalization and tax rolls; the old scouts, with a half-century of Mary Elizabeth memories; the new scouts, with dreams of a new camp not on the way to the mall; the conservationists, with dreams of securing the survival of the largest piece of open land in the city for green space; and the developer in the wings, with plans and construction permits.

—

We park the van, squeeze past the gate, and finally enter the surprising sanctuary of Mary Elizabeth. The distance from Spartanburg is greater than I would have imagined. There are birdcalls. Water runs over stones. And for 360 degrees, through a trick of perspective and topography, I can't see a house, even though the hardwoods are still leafless. "As you can see, the creek isn't in the best of shape through here," Doug points out as we start down the slope toward the heart of the camp. I look into the woods and see what he means. The channel is deeply eroded, and the flood plain is clogged in places with weeds. There is some debris brought downstream from people's yards. I think for a moment there is something tragic about abused land deep in a city like this, like a wild seabird coated with petroleum after an oil spill.

Gerald puts his glasses to his eyes for the first time, something flitting below us. We walk the main road a hundred yards, dropping quickly down to Holston Creek which flows northeast toward confluence with Fairforest Creek soon after it crosses Ezell Boulevard. Doug says the camp makes for a nice outdoor laboratory so close to school.

I have other motives. I listen to Doug talk about the endangered flower we'll see. I want to know about the plant, but I see it as a powerful ally in any fight that might come to save Mary Elizabeth. I'm hoping that my knowledge of the plant, if communicated to the right people, can help in mounting a fight to save the fifty-year-old camp from sale and eventual development.

As we descend into the camp, we can see the old lodge perched on the hillside above the creek, a ropes course beyond, and two or three picnic shelters. We pass a bog that the Girl Scouts have tried to fill in with brush. The area, probably saturated by a nearby spring, bubbles rusty water, and the brush is rotting. "Now there's an example of how I would maybe do things different," Doug says. "I'd let this bog develop."

I look around me in every direction. It's true what everyone says. This is as close to the mountains as it gets in the Piedmont. Through this long, narrow draw, Holston Creek has deeply creased the land. The creek is broken every twenty feet by a tiny rapid with strong flow, creating mountainlike drop pools and eddies. There is topography here. Standing next to the creek, which is noisy with falling water, it is possible to believe that Spartanburg—and the sprawling mall less than a mile away—does not exist.

Restoration is possible. It would take hard work and commitment, but the Mary Elizabeth Woods could be a model urban forest preserve. There are some big white oaks on the ridges. These big trees predate the camp, and the younger hardwoods and pines have thrived undisturbed for fifty years. If the camp is developed as a gated community, I will not have access to this creek, these trees. I will always be a trespasser, as I am today.

I begin to talk about how I'd like to see the land used if it is sold by the Girl Scouts. "I'd like to see a college like Wofford or some conservation organization buy it and turn it into a restoration ecology lab," I say. "I'd get the community working on restoring this forest, planting native trees, removing species that are intrusive. I'd work to restore the forest to the same diversity and richness it had when the first settlers arrived. Fifty years from now I'd like to see every school group in the county brought here to see what a Piedmont hardwood forest with old growth looks like." I say that we don't need another housing development, but we sure need a forest preserve to teach our children how a landscape—even a landscape as depleted and abused as the South Carolina Piedmont—can recover, can even flourish.

"It would take a lot of restoration. It's a pretty damaged system," Doug says. "The soils of the Piedmont have been so depleted. This creek has a pretty big watershed, and it gets runoff from all the development west of here, so the water quality is not that good."

"But it could be recovered," I argue. "Recovery. That would be visionary. That would be better than houses down in here. Better than lawns, carports, and mulch."

I ask about a sign that says AREA PRONE TO FLASH FLOOD. We cross a little bridge and Doug laughs, tells us a story about being down in here once and crossing this bridge during a thunderstorm and then, moments later, seeing the little bridge carried past him by rising water. "It really turns into a funnel down here when that runoff gets up a head of steam."

We stand on the bridge for a few minutes and look down at the water. Water skates drift back and forth on the surface of the little pool. "See their shadows?" Doug points out. He explains how the insects look as if they are suspended on the water by their skinny legs alone, but their shadows reflect on the bottom sand and reveal how each creature is actually floating on a web of tiny hairs. Each tiny "foot" looks like a fuzzy black cotton ball reversed in its shadow. "Little moments like this, that's what's wonderful about natural history," Doug says.

A little farther down the trail Doug leans over and points to a small-leafed, green flower growing in a patch of maybe ten plants along a drainage-ditch bank. "That's it guys, the dwarf-flowered heartleaf." The tiny plant is peeking out from among dry leaves. It is beautiful and fragile, so emblematic of what's left of the original Piedmont landscape. Doug brushes a few crumbled leaves away, exposing the tiny, colorless flowers close to the roots. "They bloom under the leaf mulch," Doug says. "This is one of the plants most characteristic of this area. It prefers the Pacolet sandy loam soil. It's rare but fairly widely scattered through the area."

Stephanie Mills, author of *In Service of the Wild: Restoring and Reinhabiting Damaged Land,* says "a species ... is a unique response to circumstance; a syllable of beauty." The beauty of this tiny Piedmont flower is that it's hidden. It, like Camp Mary Elizabeth, flourishes only as long as it does not push up into the light. For fifty years what has kept this place a sanctuary is how, through some stroke of fate and stewardship, the world grew up ugly and busy around it.

Now market forces want to bring the business of the world close by. As we walk back to Doug's van I am sullen and quiet with the reality of the work ahead. I know that if the Mary Elizabeth Woods is to be saved from development and commerce, it will take hard work, long hours, and diligence. It will take changing a community's focus, maybe even its values. It will take us all slowing down, leaning over, looking below, seeing hidden things, important things that pass quickly without notice. And yes, unfortunately, it will also take money, since the Girl Scouts seem bent on building their "dream camp," and the abandoned Mary Elizabeth isn't it.

Behind me, Doug and Gerald note a quick rush of warblers moving through the underbrush. Gerald turns back, lifts his glasses to make one more identification. All I can think of is the dwarf-flowered heartleaf and its steady presence, a "syllable of beauty." When we get to Ezell Boulevard, we wait minutes before we can slip back into the city-bound traffic. The car horns break the last of the woodland silence, and the dwarf-flowered heartleaf recedes into memory. Who can utter a plea, shaped from such syllables, to save a place like Camp Mary Elizabeth?

The
Road

Four property owners come to Frank's front porch for the founding of the Sampler Drive Association. Frank hands me a legal pad when I reach the top of the steps. "John, you're an English professor," he says. "You can keep the minutes." I settle on the porch swing as the meeting begins. The other three men—Eddie, Frank, and Vernon—sit in patio chairs. We are at 3,500 feet in western North Carolina, and I stare out at the distant Nantahala Range, the sublime view at the top of the long, difficult gravel road we are finally organizing to maintain. It's the birth of our small mountain community, I think to myself with some sadness.

My sadness is at odds with settlement. It grows from the understanding that has brought us together, not some high ideal—faith, hope, charity. Before today we were a loosely connected group with four separate lives on the mountain. We were not neighbors as much as acquaintances. The road has been there under us—with the exception of Frank, who has known it longer—from the day each of us bought our property, and we and our friends have all traveled it. The road will now be at the center of our association. Receding ranges of blue mountains, endless falling water, and ample sky surround us, but it is this steep and demanding road that is bonding us on this summer afternoon.

I'm not into maintenance. I think it best not to admit this to the group, but the quality of the road has never mattered much to me. All my life I have not been much of a maintainer. I know it is one of my social failures, but I claim no perfection, nor do I yearn for it. I let grass grow too long and watch as roofs get holes and as vehicles and tools rust before their time through neglect and wear. Sometimes I don't notice things close at hand. Other times I am so fixed on what is close by that I lose the sense of passing time and its ravages. Frank doesn't know I would have driven to my property, good road or not, because I love just being there. My visiting friends have been mostly limited to the ones who own 4x4s. I have never put much thought into who was maintaining the road, and I think I could honestly say that I would not complain if climbing the road to my property were more like a truck contest on the Extreme Sports Channel. I know the sprawling story of literature intimately, but the whole long history of engineering is lost on me. Speed has never impressed me. Convenience is not very often an essential. Why did we send a man to the moon? I often ask when pushed into a corner about modern life. What did it prove? How did it improve the essential life of my time?

I guess it all falls on the meaning of that word: essential. For Frank, and many men and women, maintenance of those things that keep our lives "civil" is essential. Frank might argue that it's "deadbeats" like me who expect others to do the maintenance while we lie around in the hammock hidden away in hollows and think. Does he realize it would take a long time before I noticed? As my emotional reflection peaks, Frank calls the meeting to order. I remind myself that what we are doing in our meeting is simply formalizing a certain level of expectation that already exists for the road, that is already agreed on. It's obvious I'm not sure how I feel about that. It's not settled with me. Most of civilization's basic services have not reached back into my little hidden hollow. Should the road be maintained or not? Should *status quo* for the road be whether Frank's sedan could easily make it to the top? Should we only occasionally do some work to keep it from turning into ruts, ridges, and run-off? And why did Frank name it "Sampler Drive" when the county approached him about a name for the green road sign at the bottom? Why not ask the poet over the ridge to suggest something more local, more rustic?

I've driven some bad roads—in Mexico I once followed a friend down a dry riverbed for almost twenty miles. She broke an axle and we each had to fix a flat tire. We came out the other end in fine shape with an adventure under our remaining tires. I think that even at its worst our road would still be better than that one. And didn't a friend's husband once drive a Buick Park Avenue to the bottom of my drive, a place where I was told only 4x4s should venture? Once my power pole (I do have electricity—surely now one of civilization's givens, even for me) was struck by lightning, and I warned the electrician that he may consider my road impassable. He brought his tiny pickup to the bottom of the drive, jumped out, and said, "This ain't no bad road."

Bad road or not, my property is at what I hope will always be the end of the road. In what would pass for the logic of inaccessibility, I am the one with the most to be thankful for, the most distance to travel from the paved road three-quarters of a mile away. But I know a little of the ancient history of this particular road, and it helps to color this meeting for me. Thomas, the friend I bought my place from, actually predates Frank on the mountain. Thomas has told me stories of driving the road in the early eighties in an old Oldsmobile station wagon when what is now Frank's road was really no more than a logging road, a two-track pushed up the mountain to skid out timber and hopefully open a few impressive views. Back then, in the Ur-years of the road, every third or fourth trip up to the property Thomas would get his car stuck and have to walk back to John's Creek Road to find the man who sold him the property to pull the station wagon over some enormous rut with his truck.

Driving that bad road for Thomas was better than walking, but not much better. He was poor—the property he owned on the mountain was his only real asset—so he saw no need to worry about whether a road had ruts. Thomas planned to live on the property someday, but he didn't plan on using the road, which, after ascending to the ridge's crest from John's Creek, dropped down into his property (now my property) from above. Thomas planned to open a second old logging road that came in off John's Creek. He'd checked and he had the right-of-way. As Thomas figured it, the second road wouldn't have as much of a grade and was a half mile shorter.

I met Frank the summer Thomas sold me the property. The first thing I did on visiting my new property was get my Mazda pickup stuck at the bottom of the steep drive. Thank goodness Thomas was with me, and I dispatched him for help. Thomas walked to Frank's house and asked him to pull me out with his tractor. "If you're gonna live back here, you need to buy a 4X4," Frank advised me as the tractor cleared the top of the ridge with my gray pickup. I could see there was a great contrast between my Florida summer resident, Frank, riding off on his old, red tractor, and Thomas, my Celtic anarchist poet friend, who had sold me this little piece of mountain paradise. If I wasn't going to fix my road, I could at least afford to buy a new truck.

After I purchased my Toyota 4X4, I wanted to use it. When I drove up from Spartanburg, I'd always begin to get excited when I turned off State Highway 107 and headed up two-lane Caney Fork Road. After six miles I'd turn off Caney Fork and onto John's Creek, a paved road with a short history (Thomas says it was still gravel when he bought the property) and a little less clearance on the sides and a little more gradient. But it was when I turned off John's Creek onto Sampler Drive that my heart actually beat faster. After winter rains had deeply creased the steep sections of the drive, I had to lock the hubs to get to the top of the ridge. This was the contrast I was looking for with my city life, something real, something palpable as four-wheel drive.

For five years I have passed Frank's house each time I head over the ridge to drop down into my little secluded hollow. The house on the ridge somehow strikes me as an extension of his former life in Florida, not really a place of retreat. They spend eight months a year now on Sampler Drive, but is this home really different from a house on a street outside of Ocala? What I was after was escape from the grids and pavement of city planners. Frank seemed to want mostly what he had at home. Conveniences, plus the view. I knew that up in the big house on the hill Frank had television, a washer and dryer, a telephone, a dishwasher, and even a complete woodworking shop in the basement. He had graciously had me up to dinner on several occasions. I enjoyed his company, but I was troubled deeply at the encroaching civility.

I know I sound a little like Ted Kaczynski, but maybe there is an escapist deep in many of us, especially the males. To want to get away is one thing—to want to send letter bombs is another. Maybe there is some guy ready, like Horace Kepart, to get on a train and leave family and friends, to end up living "off the grid" in some sleepy hollow. Maybe there is a deep ecoterrorist ready to blow up the future, sick of the present with its bills, machines, and responsibilities. The theme arises often enough in our great American literature—Washington Irving's "Rip Van Winkle," James Fenimore Cooper's Leather-Stocking Tales, and of course old Henry David Thoreau. Did it ever occur to Frank that he might have a potential Thoreau living over the ridge and that his maintenance road program might be stunting a great work of literature? Did Frank realize that the road would probably remain in ruin if he did not restore it to his notion of service, what I'll call the Buick test? Did he know that Thomas, the happy anarchist, the crusty Celtic, the devout druid would have never taken an interest in the road, that he had been planning on bypassing the road entirely by coming in underneath the Florida ridge people? And when did Frank know that I was different, susceptible to his overtures of community, organization, and association? These are the thoughts that pooled about me as I began to take notes on the Sampler Drive Association's first meeting.

It's hard to keep up with all the twists and turns of the road, which I can see just below us if I drop my occasional gaze from the mountain distances. There is a particular turn in the road where Frank thinks we need to do some blasting to deepen a ditch. I never realized there was so much engineering involved in something as simple as a road down a mountain. I feel inadequate but soon become aware that everyone has his limits when it comes to building. "I've never worked with dynamite," Eddie says, shaking his head.

"I've blown a few stumps out of the ground in Florida," Vernon adds.

"Well, it's agreed then. We'll probably need to get a road man to do some blasting for us when it's needed," Frank says. "I'll show you where when we drive the road."

Frank is in white leisure shorts. He has his shoes off, and his toes are those of a man who has worn serious work shoes a long time— nails discolored or missing altogether. I don't know what he did for a living, but I know he's worked with his hands. His right index finger is missing, and the next two nails have been shaved off by a close call. Sawmill? Packing machine? He wastes no time, speaks his mind as if this conversation has been percolating within him for ten years. He explains how the road has served him well through- out his mountain retirement, how it has delivered his 4x4 truck and his sedan to the top of the ridge, assuring access to his good view. He makes it clear, though, that he is now ready to pass on the respon- sibility for maintenance of the road. He wants no mistakes made about that. It has cost him thousands of dollars and as many hours to keep the road in good shape for the dozen years he has had a house on the ridge top. "What's past is past," he says, dismissing all the hard work that has gone into maintaining the road. Then, he outlines the work he thinks needs to be shared to maintain the road from now on—cleaning out the ditches, digging some news ones, replacing several culverts. He figures that if each of us contributes one hundred dollars up front, then for twenty-five dollars a month we can keep the road in good shape. Frank says he has talked to the other four owners on the mountain and all have agreed to con- tribute to the fund. "We need a president," Frank says. I nominate Eddie and he is the unanimous choice.

We've elected Eddie because everybody knows he has plans to build a big log house high on the ridge top. The winter before, Eddie had spent thousands widening the last few hundred yards of the road past Vernon's cabin, then pushing a driveway straight up the mountainside until it topped the ridge and flattened out in a west-facing view. I'd driven up from Spartanburg midwinter to be greeted by Eddie's "improvements." My first reaction had been anger—my mountain solitude further eroded by another neighbor, but I soon got used to the good road continuing another few hundred yards toward my place, widened, crowned, topped with crushed rock and road bond. "Who knows what we'll have in twenty years," he laughs after we've voted. "We might have an interstate coming right through here."

I cringe, but I like Eddie and his endless all-American optimism. He has the credibility success brings (he is a citrus grower from south Florida), and I have to admit his plan for a three-thousand-square-foot ridge-top summer house shows a certain commitment. There is no doubt about Frank. His house is substantial, though not showy. And Vernon has spent the summer putting up a small cabin on his view lot. They've all seen my place, four acres of secluded hollow at the end of a down-tending logging road. They know I never trim back the blackberry cane, drive a six-year-old Toyota truck, live in a two-story octagonal tower with no indoor plumbing, and ignore how the water carves deep ruts in what passes for a driveway. They know who should be president.

For some reason I nearly quote the poet A. R. Ammons—"If anything will level with you water will"—but think better of it. I don't want to drain away what little credibility I have channeled with my first elected community office, vice-president/secretary of the Sampler Drive Association. I've kept my mouth shut for the most part, and they have no idea what wild ideas are teeming in my brain. I feel some residual male guilt, though—some impulse a Roman centurion might have understood—and search my memory for a reference to velocity or such, but come up blank. The closest thing I can engineer for conversation is the Coriolis effect, but I can't remember whether that is why water goes down the drain in one or the other circular direction or whether that is how wind blows faster past skyscrapers.

Despite the voices of the anarchists in my head, I know there are more of us on the mountain now, and I have to admit Frank is probably right. It is time for us to organize, to take some of the load off his seventy-four year-old body. He's fought the good fight against the elements. He's shoveled enough gravel, cleaned enough ditches, built enough water breaks. But what about freedom? What about beholding to no one? What about disappearing into your hollow and drinking beer and throwing the bottles under a cedar tree? The anarchist cries out, and I want to get up and leave the meeting, get my hound dog and hightail it over the ridge and leave these men to curse me as I drive the road to my place. I know they can't stop me. I've got a right-of-way. But instead of acting out I sit quietly and take notes as Frank tells us how it will be: Eddie's wife will be treasurer, and we elect her in spite of her absence. Frank decides that Eddie will drive into town and open a checking account on Monday before he returns to Florida. With the business part over, Vernon picks up his walking stick and strolls back down the steps. Doesn't he want to accompany us on our ride to the bottom of the hill? Eddie asks. No, he has to help his wife pack for a return trip to Florida on Monday. "I'll leave the briefing to Frank," Vernon says, beginning his walk down the ridge.

We descend the road in a series of sharp but serviceable switchbacks past several view lots. Someone once told me that the way they used to lay out a road in the old days was to take a pig to the ridge top and turn it loose. Whatever route the pig took down was the route they'd take. I wonder if the first architects of the road had taken a similar approach. I think it best not to compare the road to a pig path as Frank points out all the problem spots on our three-quarters of a mile of steep gravel. Frank recites the checklist of spots where the road has a tendency to washboard, where the bedrock hinders a good ditch, where the gravel washes in the sheet run-off after intense summer storms. He talks about crowns, water breaks, and the advantages of plastic culverts over metal ones. As we descend the road, I draw a detailed map on the legal pad. Eddie looks over and laughs, wonders out loud what possible good such a little map could be.

I've seen surviving Roman roads laid out in grids on hiking maps in England. They stretch for hundreds of miles in straight lines with so little grade Frank could only dream it in this mountain country. It was all mathematics, which they were good at. Legions could move efficiently over long distances. Many of today's best long-distance hiking trails follow the old Roman roads, and a millennium's neglect makes us forget how perfectly engineered they once were. Eisenhower had the same thing in mind with our interstate system, our own nod toward the efficiency of empire.

Now, the old Roman roads look more like the two-track leading down into my property, angling off Eddie's newly spread gravel. Why have these good roads? Most of my neighbors would argue, "Because we can." To fall back to ruts and rises is to give into our most barbarian urges. Thomas would laugh and point to the small path leading into my property that predates all the roads, even the logging roads.

I like to speculate how Uncle Bob Brown used to walk out of the hollow on a narrow footpath that hugged the hillside all the way to John's Creek, a half mile below. The path probably predated him, going back to the Cherokees or further. "Locals don't need such good roads. They never live on the ridge tops," one local told me. "The Florida people do." Thomas likes to tell how when he was looking for land, the owner kept showing him "view lots." Finally, Thomas got it through to the old mountain man: he wasn't a Florida person. He wanted a place with water, a place flat enough to plant a garden. He wanted some place he could settle. Down in the hollow Thomas finally found the old cabin ruins that would one day become a home site. That the road came over the ridge and dropped five hundred feet into the hollow was simply a convenience at the time Thomas bought it. He had no intention of driving up to go down forever.

Eddie slows for a particularly sharp curve and Frank points out a water break, three 2x4s nailed to form a trough for water to run quickly off the road. "When I was putting in that break, Thomas came down from his place in that little truck. He couldn't get through and I refused to move my truck. I told him he was at least going to help me with this one and he said he couldn't because he had a bad back. Well, I went right on banging away with that pickax. He was mad, but he got out of the truck and helped."

I wonder whether Frank is telling this story especially for me. He knows Thomas and I are close friends, and I've spent only a few days working on the road. I laugh at my friend's expense, and we drive on, listening as Frank tells us where he thinks we should ditch, where a culvert is stopped up, where a water break is beyond repair. "Isn't this where I saw you last winter fighting with all that water running in the road?" Eddie asks.

"About five hundred gallons a minute ran through here," Frank says. "Remember, the key to a good road is keeping the water out of the middle of it."

"I wish I knew more about water," my soon-to-be neighbor Eddie says, sounding like a civil engineer in training, as we approach the bottom of the steep gravel road in his blue SUV with the creamy leather seats. I'm glad one of us has the head for it. I'll pay my twenty-five dollars per month and the association can sign me up for shoveling out ditches in November.

Walking
Kelsey
Creek

I'm cutting through the crumbling pinewoods to the northwest of Kelsey Creek with my friend Gerald. This section of the creek flows through Camp Croft State Park in southern Spartanburg County, in the Piedmont of South Carolina. On Sunday afternoon walks like this one we leave the truck along Dairy Ridge Road. Once parked there it's either cross the ditch and enter the pinewoods or wrestle the eager dogs on leashes down to the concrete bridge and enter the woods where the overgrown trail follows the creek along the remnants of a nineteenth century millrace.

We choose the pines this time, the four dogs soon off their leashes, noses to ground safely ahead of us. Gerald hates pine trees, but we try to slow down enough to look and listen, just as we would among oaks and poplar. After all, we are in the woods, Gerald says, and it's better than anything Spartanburg's city limits has to offer on a Sunday afternoon. We love to be outdoors, especially in late summer with the fresh memory of South Carolina heat finally beginning to fade. We want green over our heads and suburbs no more than a memory. We want wilderness, but with jobs and responsibilities tugging at our tee shirts we will have to substitute a walk in the state park.

Croft is not a wilderness, but it's as close as we can get a few minutes drive from home. Croft is the county's largest green space, a state park with twenty-one miles of horse trails, mountain-bike paths, and two lakes. These are not the reasons we visit, though. We're here to dream and to walk in the woods. It's said that between the drainages of the Pacolet and Tyger Rivers, the Lawson's Fork and Fairforest Creek, there grew hardwoods ten feet around at their base. And the streams ran clear, even after a heavy rain. When I want a feeling of what the old-growth forest must have looked like, I drive the park road to the Twin Oaks Shelter and let my imagination fill the county with trees as big as the oak in the front of the picnic shelter.

There are a few Twin Oaks Shelter–sized trees in Camp Croft, shadow trees from the time before the upstate was cut—and cut again. Now second- and third-growth hardwoods are slowly making a natural comeback on the banks of Kelsey Creek, and that's what we're heading for on this September Sunday. I keep thinking: keep the god-awful developers away; give the trees an undisturbed two hundred years, and my great-great-grandchildren might walk under giant trees again, now only available in my imagination.

But keeping developers away in Spartanburg County is a little like wishing the kudzu would vanish. Spartanburg County grows developers the way it used to grow big hardwoods. I don't think they are going to disappear the way the hardwood did, though. It seems nothing is safe or sacred if there's money to be made in the upstate. Sometimes when I'm in the woods, surrounded by the humming, hazy distances with the rotting remnants of human mediation out of sight, I believe for a moment that if we could bring the developers here, even they could be convinced to leave this little corner of the county out of their formulas for sewer service and subdivision. But it seems every year I hear rumors of someone salivating to develop Camp Croft, pull the land from the public trust and "privatize" it.

I've seen what private ownership does for land deemed "valuable," and I'm not interested in giving Spartanburg's free-market-minded a shot at it. Leave the land to vegetable riot and rot. I'll sit back, walking here ten or twenty times a year, hoping the first growth will return. For now, Gerald and I will have to make do with second-, third-, fourth-, or even fifth-growth forest.

"Here's a true story, John," Gerald said as we walked into Camp Croft. "I stopped at the South Carolina rest station on the interstate between here and Georgia. There used to be a good stand of hardwoods where I would walk when I stopped. But last time I stopped, someone had knocked them all down. I was mad and I went down and confronted the woman working at the information booth. 'Why did you cut all the trees down?' I asked. 'Oh, we needed a place to park the sixteen wheelers. But we left plenty of pines,' she said, pointing toward the cornrows of loblollies."

"'Pines? Pines,' I said. 'That's, that's just vegetable crap,'" Gerald explained, getting so angry as he remembered the woman's words that I thought he was going to pull out a sapling and light out through the woods, terrorizing rest area ghosts in the heat haze.

Pines make me feel that way too. But these Camp Croft pine-woods are volunteer, not planted, and burnt dry and dusty by a too-long summer. Fallen short-needled pine logs as thick as cannon with large, curving bark slabs sloughed off in a quick dry rot lie everywhere. The tan heart of each fallen log is eaten by insects and laced with the runs of pine beetles. Gerald calms down and says that if I'm quiet I'll hear the pine beetle larvae chewing in the dead logs. To me the markings of their work look like someone trying to make up a new alphabet. For a moment, even though they're pines, the woods are beautiful and quiet. Hard as I listen, I can't hear the beetles.

As we bushwhack southeast, I notice the forest floor is patterned with sheet-wash deposits, tiny fences of broken needles and rotted wood running at odd angles on the red clay. These are the land's last picket lines against heavy erosion. This damaged land, where a thin sheen of dead pine needles and Virginia creeper doesn't cover it, is rock-hard, red Piedmont clay. Left to its own devices, the land in Camp Croft naturally says topsoil, thick loam, oak, and poplar. But here where we walk, farming and war got heavily in the way.

The woods slope toward the creek and an eroding deer trail drops from the wreckage of the pine-forest floor toward a drainage ditch where a trickle of greasy water seeps through exposed stones below. I wouldn't want to drink this water, so close to the petroleum tank fields that sprouted in Spartanburg's economic boom when the army camp moved out fifty years ago. There was a time in the six-ties when the government wasn't so interested in liberal things like environmental protection and emissions standards, when Kelsey Creek caught on fire and burned like an oil spill because of leakage from the tank fields near its headwaters. Today the creek water runs cleaner, clear enough to swim in, and there are even reports of beaver back in the park.

I hate development the irrational way Gerald hates pine trees. I've never understood how the whole continent fell slowly under the twin shadows of utility and greed. There's a fantasy I've had many times while standing in parks like this: what if some colonial misfit, some oddball upstate settler, had received one of those huge king's grants, and instead of cutting down all the trees and farming, he'd set it off in perpetuity as wildland? One percent of the land in the lower forty-eight states can be described as "wild" now, five hundred years after Columbus landed. Maybe in a hundred years Camp Croft will add a few thousand acres to the total.

And if Croft is ever cleared and subdivided, sweetening some developer's bank account? So much would be lost. Where would we go on a Sunday afternoon to walk the dogs, to look for snakes, or to speculate on the past, present, and future? As we walk, Gerald tells me two more Camp Croft anecdotes: at one time they wanted to put an insane asylum here in the middle of the park and out on its perimeter is a huge county landfill. It seems the park has been assaulted from all sides. I listen for the gurgling of the creek, pretend it's running clear in some early explorer's ear.

We cross where the deer cross and follow the small hoof tracks that look like embracing half moons and begin our descent toward Kelsey Creek. "Let's get over to the hardwoods on the other side of the creek," Gerald says. "God, I hate these pines." Gerald's a good friend, so I follow. I look up at the blue South Carolina sky through the pine boughs and wonder if it was that blue when the first European walked here or if that's some effect of fluorocarbons.

Much has happened to this land in the past two hundred years. The park is crisscrossed by forgotten roads, some dating back to the eighteenth and nineteenth centuries, some built to accommodate the army during the twentieth century. Most of the land was farmed at one time—cotton and corn—and wandering through the woods we've come across many standing chimneys. Once, in early spring we stumbled upon an abandoned homesite at the intersection of the overgrown remains of two roads. The big chimney shaded the outline of a flowerbed where an old-fashioned kind of white daffodil bloomed.

Where we cross, the creek is still bold from rains the week before, and when we're in sight, we realize we've entered the hardwoods at one of our favorite scenic spots, the old bridge crossing and the rabble of stones and falling water. The iron frame still stands, missing the planks of the roadbed. We cross the creek below the flaking silver ruin on ribs of exposed gneiss, one of the county's most common bedrocks.

Gerald is happier in the hardwoods on the other side. He stops, looks around, says he can feel fall coming on. "It's that dead late-summer time," he smiles. "There aren't even any birds moving through." I listen for a moment. He's right. All I hear is the creek breaking over rocks just below the old mill site and its broken cofferdam and the cars crossing on Dairy Ridge Road. These people in their cars are completely unaware there are explorers in the woods to their south. They probably don't even know where north is.

Most of the time we know where east is, and we like to leave the trail. We continue our hike by traversing an old county roadbed now thick with hardwood saplings and rotted leaves. To the south is a steep hardwood ridge above the soft floodplain thick with cane. Some of the oaks look to be over seventy years old, old enough to have felt the concussion of mortar rounds, the impact of M-1 rounds between 1942 and 1945 when Camp Croft was the largest army infantry training camp on the East Coast.

One local botanist had speculated that the older trees have enough metal in them to make chainsawing any of them dangerous to the sawyer. It's an unexpected government kind of "monkey wrenching," the tree-spiking methods so popular in the eighties out west as a means of stopping development. I turn, squint just right, and imagine the road carrying Jeeps and half-tracks, boys who would die at Anzio, Omaha Beach, the Battle of the Bulge.

Soon we notice the orange flagging, see the red survey stakes. We know the war isn't over yet. Demolition teams are covering quadrangles of the park, looking for unexploded ordinance, mortar shells, grenades. When I was a boy in the early 1960s, each summer brought a new story of a local kid losing a hand to an exploding grenade at Camp Croft. Now, fifty years after the close of the war, the government is spending thousands to try to clean it up. How well they clean it depends on plans for the park. The more development that is planned for the land, the deeper the probe needs to go. Gerald explains the flagging means they've found some piece of metal with their detectors. "Now there's a poetic image for you," Gerald laughs. "Almost a haiku: orange flagging / and mortar shells / among summer hardwoods."

Soon we turn our hardwood ramble back toward the creek, and what we call the Narrows, a spot where bedrock causes a small series of rapids. We like to sit there—and even swim in the swirling narrow pools if it's hot enough. The place has a history for us. We tell stories about it. Once, Gerald was sitting there and looked up to see a great horned owl peering down at him.

The Narrows is a place where we lie down on the warm gneiss and let it penetrate our bodies and let our minds wander free and where we speculate about things. It's the best place in Spartanburg County to sit and imagine what the woods would have looked like two hundred years before we were born. Would we have seen fish spawning in Kelsey Creek? Would oaks and poplars have arched a hundred feet above us? When was the last time a cougar walked this creek looking for deer, elk, or buffalo crossings? Or a hunting party of Cherokee walked it, down from the mountains? And who the hell was Kelsey anyway?

We also like to speculate about how bad the traffic will become on Spartanburg's west side, whether the city fathers and mothers will cut down the trees in the middle of Ezell Boulevard, and whether the downtown will ever thrive again. These questions would never come to mind if these trails were to become paved sub-division roads and Camp Croft another figure in the tax base.

Now the sun is going down, and we can feel the tugs of our separate responsibilities. Confident we've renewed our bond to one of our county's wildest spots, we call back the dogs, all four splashing in the creek downstream.

The poet Gary Snyder says "The real work is becoming native in your heart, coming to understand we really live here, that this is really the continent we're on and that our loyalties are here." I tell Gerald what Snyder says, or at least a close paraphrase, and he thinks about the poet's words as we begin walking.

"Snyder said native in your heart?" Gerald says as we head back for the truck. "I just hope there aren't any pine trees in my heart."

Huxley

When I was still

caught up in this dream of

a static, age-old existence,

I suddenly thought of

my pocket watch. . . .

—Carl Jung,

Memories, Dreams,

Reflections

One day this summer I think of Aldous Huxley on his first mesca-
line trip. Another day I walk up my driveway to the pretty place on
the ridge above the tower; there's plenty of time for turkey tracks in
the sand; a brown fence lizard, a guest from the Paleozoic, jutting
under a rock when I pass; and three new wildflowers blooming: the
first black-eyed Susans, spotted wintergreen in the shadows, and a
new aster in full sun.

There is time to see the rutted road, a grand canyon for ants carrying the carapace of a deerfly to their nest in the old poplar stump.
There is, as always, time to linger at the view lot, lost in a descend-
ing bowl of transverse ridges for twenty miles.

Then I hear my neighbor Frank start his pickup just over the
ridge, and I remember I've promised him I would help with some
driveway maintenance, and there isn't so much time now.

"How does tomorrow look?" I ask, walking up.

"Tomorrow, for what?" he answers from his truck window.

"The day for weed-eating the drive," I say.

"Not too good. No, not too good at all," Frank says, sounding embarrassed, not at his answer, but that I'd asked, embarrassed for me
and my lost day. "Tomorrow is Sunday."

"Sunday? Isn't today Friday?"

"It's Saturday."

"I could have sworn it was Friday," I say, glancing down.

"It's July 6," he says. "So it's Saturday all day."

Another day like all the others and I am reading. It is the fall of 1860, and while Sumter and Manassas are ripening, Henry David Thoreau is thinking about an old-growth stand of oaks called Inches Wood, near Boxboro, and goes to walk there. He measures every tree he passes and in so doing records, "a black oak ten feet [in] circumference, trunk tall and of regular form . . ." During these years, Thoreau walked four hours a day.

And then I am reading a Cherokee chant for "making them forget, to lessen argument":

Now! *Ha!* It was our Mother in front of You & me: a smooth tree leaf.

You and I have just come to cut the eyes and the souls of the people in the seven clans districts.

A great wind has just thundered over our souls for times.

Thought has just descended in a column, face-downward, and has just joined their souls that have just sunk into the sea.

Another day I remember that cicadas know when to sing by temperature. Another, I read Thoreau again: "On the north end, also, the first evidence we had that we were coming out of the wood— approaching its border—was the crowing of a cock."

And then another, I make a list of all the ways to figure time: Light. Dark. The path the sun makes across the sky. The cycle of the seasons: spring, summer, fall, winter, spring, summer, fall, winter. The rise and fall of groundwater run-off. Tracking the stars and planets, their disappearance and appearance. The mating, migration, and molting of animals. The blooming of flowers. The falling temperature. The rising sap. The regularity of storms. The absence of storms. Warblers in the morning. Owls near evening, continuing until morning.

The body's clock. Internal rhythms like heartbeat, breath, and the function of the kidneys and bowels. Youth to old age. Growing grayer, growing shorter. The sagging muscle. The dimming eyesight. The failing teeth. The shrinking prostate. The falling erection.

Crops maturing. Planting-time. Harvesttime. Milking-time. Calendar. Gregorian. Julian. Liberian. Newgate. Mayan. Circles within circles. The Long Count. Reckoning the days. Sunday. Monday. Tuesday. Wednesday. Thursday. Friday. Saturday. The regularity of a schedule. Account book. Fixed beginning. Duration. Subdivision. Adjustments. Leap years and blue moons. Cockcrow. Chinese water clock. Sundial. Mechanical clock. Time clock. Atomic clock. Digital wristwatch. Day-Timer.

Another day over forty, and I long to balance my days. No more swerving off into sand paths with *No Outlet* signs. Enough of that, not to end up the speaker in Roethke's "The Far Field," who dreams the road "ending at last in a hopeless sand-rut, / Where the car stalls, / Churning in a snowdrift / Until the headlights darken."

No, none of that for me. I'll fix my road today and help Frank too. I'll build a bathhouse. Chop back the new growth to reclaim my clearing. I'll find the time to be both practical as well as intellectual. Three hours writing early today, and three sweating with the sling blade. The rest spent reading and preparing food, sleeping. But soul work is an unpredictable thing, full of sand ruts and detours along the way. Such as picking up a book, another day, and Roethke is part of the detour again:

—Or to lie naked in sand,
In the silted shallows of a slow river,
Fingering a shell,
Thinking:
Once I was something like this, mindless,
Or perhaps with another mind, less peculiar;
Or to sink down to the hips in a mossy quagmire;
Or, with skinny knees, to sit astride a wet log,
Believing:

Today the road isn't fixed. The bathhouse isn't started. The weeds stand like lions' manes, uncut in the breeze, so after lunch I start another project, go down the mountain to buy an unfinished wooden screen door, a simple thing, probably take a day to find in town, to hang, to varnish.

Crawling out in my 4X4, I'm blocked by the septic tank crew at the pretty place on the ridge. They want to talk, to stop working, to take a break, the backhoe silent for a minute on this hot summer day. Amazed somebody lives "back in there," they want to know how long I go without seeing anyone.

"Days," I say.

"Hot, ain't it?" one says in a neighborly way, as if to offer me what they perceive is needed human contact.

"Not half as hot as it is behind that backhoe," I say.

"Shit, this ain't nothing now. We got to sink this pipe by hand. That'll be something to watch in this heat. You ought to come up and help us. A little work will do you good. Stop spending so much time with yourself."

The very local hardware store is a trip back to village life: lawn tools, seeds, nails, hammers, and odd-length boards.

"Ah, a screen door? You mean like a regular screen door, neighbor?"

"Yes, a regular screen door."

"No, no sir-re. We sure don't have none of them."

"Is there another hardware?"

"Yes, yes sir-re. Ace Hardware, on the backstreet, downtown. They'll have your screen door if anybody would."

At Ace, the man, wearing red and white corporate colors, heads out from behind the counter when I come in. Ace is the place, and this the "helpful hardware man."

"Yes sir, what can we help you with today?"

"I need a screen door."

"We might be able to help you with that. They come thirty-three and thirty-six."

"I'll need a six-foot-six by thirty-three inches."

We go out the door and down the building's side to where two teenage boys in sweaty tees are moving railroad ties with a forklift into a shed.

"Looks like we got mostly thirty-six inchers, but we might be able to find a thirty-three or two. Todd, you seen my tape?"

"I ain't seen your tape but I seen mine." He pats his hip, where the yellow tape measure rides. "I seen it right here since morning."

"Well, I believe you seen mine too yesterday."

"But today it seems your tape's done gone."

"Well, I'll borrow yours then. This gentleman is looking for a screen door."

"Looks like he's done found a few," the boy says, tossing the tape.

He finds nothing but thirty-sixes, whole pallets of thirty-sixes.

"Six-foot-six did you say? Well it's not your standard height for a door."

"I can always cut it off."

"That's for sure. You can always make 'em shorter. Just hard to make 'em longer."

I eye another row of wooden screen doors, stacked two deep along one wall.

"Is this one thirty-three inches?"

"Oh no. That's a thirty-six if I've ever seen one. And I've seen a lot of 'em. Can't rightly say I've seen a thirty-three right now just looking."

He checks all twenty screen doors along the wall, and the only thirty-three he finds has a hole punched in it.

"These damn boys we hire cost me every day. I told them not to unload them if they got holes poked in them."

We go back inside. He tells me, "If we had a screen door it would cost you forty-four dollars. Can you believe that? Forty-four dollars for a screen door. And that's a cheap one." That's it. He says, "Come on back anytime if you need something else."

The cicadas are already working when I pull down the drive. Then another day it's the Cherokees, back again:

Where other men live it is lonely.

They are very loathsome.

The common polecat has made them so like himself that they are fit
only for his company.

They have become mere refuse.

They are very loathsome.

The common opossum has made them so like himself that they are fit
only for his company . . .

I stand with my face toward the Sun Land.

No one is ever lonely with me.

I am very handsome.

I shall certainly be blue . . .

Your soul has come into the center of my soul, never to turn away.

Today I've been at it since sunrise, and midmorning the dog stirs from the futon and noses my typing hand. It's like the old joke about the carpenters. One asks the other, "What's the most amazing invention of all time?"

The other offers up the telephone, the car, the electric light, the atom bomb.

"Nope," the first one says. "Them's good but it's the thermos bottle."

"The thermos bottle?" the other says, holding his up.

"Yep, the thermos bottle. It keeps the hot things hot and the cold things cold. How do it know?"

One other day, not this one but one like it, we take the same morning walk, up the steep path along the creek to the spot I've cleared next to the tiny waterfall. The dog continues up the path when I stop to sit and listen. She squats and noses through the rhododendron thicket and usually flushes a ruffled grouse somewhere up there. I hear the quick, steady beat of the grouse, its rising bursting flight as it gets away each morning. I sit for a few minutes. It is too easy to say time collapses within the sound of a running mountain stream. It is more as if time folds into itself. The tensile strength of the moment is doubled when water is present; like an accordion, the moments hinge and double over.

I notice things in this accordion time I never see when I'm "down below," off the mountain. Things like the rhododendrons when they finally bloom. I've felt it for days now, the almost-bursting-forth, the genetic flower code finally ready to play itself out as bell-shaped corollas of five rounded lobes burst into pink or white bouquets.

Some days, sitting there within the sound of water, I wonder what it would be like to sit there forever, to sit all day. What would pass by? Some say that if we sit in one place long enough we'll see it all. One day I spent three hours in the hammock, just watching, not even napping. Saw the most wondrous thing. Right below me, a mole was pushing a tunnel of earth before it, and out of the loosened soil jumped earthworms crawling quickly away. Another day I saw a salamander, a red one, crawl out from under a rock and stop. I watched it for an hour and it didn't move. Then I went inside, came back out, and it was gone.

(That moment, remembered just now, in spite of the Cherokee chant against remembering, digression.)

But this day, the hottest day of the summer, I read how Roethke came to "a still, but not a deep center, / A point outside the glittering current." Go into the current, see how that feels. Deepen the rhododendron-shaded place in the creek. It's trivial work, outside the currency of clearing, maintenance.

Dig and dig in the cold water, swirling silt and pebbles with my blade, slinging shovel loads down the mossy rocks below. My feet are numb, though the air approaches ninety in the sun.

Dig out a form no bigger than a body, no deeper than my belly, strip, and lie down there on this hot day. The current flows over my brown belly, my arms fast beside me. Snorkel like a turtle. Cool down.

But the cold is also a clock. It tells me when to rise and enter the hot day and my body. If I stayed, the stream would take me deeper. Roethke again: "What I love is near at hand, / Always, in earth and air."

Temporal time is not endless. Try to remember one day. The rhododendron *does* bloom. My dog *will* nose my hand when her walking clock goes off. And yet there are those folds that Huxley slipped blissfully within.

"Where am I?" the protagonist knocked unconscious mutters at the beginning of a mystery, never "What time is it?" Place first, and then the exterior decoration of time.

Another day I remember the list of questions Huxley left for his assistant to ask as the philosopher of science wandered the orderly laboratory out of his right mind.

"There seems to be plenty of it," is what Huxley mumbled when the white-coated boy asked, "Dr. Huxley, what about time?"

Headwaters

A January cold front hauled clouds east as we finally left Spartanburg. We weren't all agreeing about time. After all, we were an hour
and a half late leaving, and it was the professors' fault. It was interim
at Wofford College, a time when students take one course. It's a period when "the lions train the lion trainer," a mentor of mine once
said. I'll admit the students often have the upper hand. They go into
the month bent on "experience," with their brakes set against the
stuff the preceding and approaching semesters are known for: difficult books, lectures, and what the faculty calls "the life of the mind,"
whatever that might mean in college today—that youth-driven
place of the Web, video games, and dorm-wide Cablevision.

Our interim project was "Black Creek: A Human and Natural
History." Watersheds have become an amateur passion of mine, and
I saw the college interim program as a chance to inflict my enthu-
siasm on a group of students. My colleague and coteacher Jim was
in finance, and he was on board for a completely different reason,
more personal and, at least in the beginning stops of the odyssey,
less evangelical. When we began our collaboration, Jim knew little
about watersheds, but he was deeply interested in Black Creek, the
blackwater stream of his childhood. He wanted to explore it and his
hometown, Hartsville, in the new context of middle age. You could
say he wanted to learn about the creek as if he were a student again.
Most of my colleagues would agree this is the true spirit of interim.
Seize on an idea, articulate a brief, intense program, and set it into
motion.

Interim is a leftover from the late sixties. Back then hundreds of
liberal arts colleges across the country carved a month or two from
their regular semester or quarter system to open an unstructured,
unrestricted space. Today, Wofford is one of only a few dozen colleges to hang on to the schedule. As we like to say at the small, liberal arts college, "Some things never change. Some things never
should." Every January it's a living anachronism. It's like seeing

Ken Kesey and his Merry Pranksters show up for a Young Republicans rally. Obviously, the students like it. It's said the interim is one of our best recruiting tools. They see it as a soft spot between the gritty millstones of traditional semesters.

I took to Wofford's interim from the beginning. As a student there in the seventies I fell right into its loose structure and leisurely expectations. I remember very little about my eight college semesters, but my four interims stand out like a ridge above low ground. I studied Indian art, designed a textbook to teach junior high children about local snakes, and traveled twice on independent projects.

It was the two travel interims like the current Black Creek project that did me in, tripped me out of the day-to-day world of college more successfully than a dose of LSD. My sophomore year I spent three weeks walking the low-tide line on Edisto Beach looking for wave-washed remains from the Pleistocene. My friend David led me into this adventure. He was a biology major and had a legitimate interest in South Carolina's vanished megafauna. He wrote up the form, satisfying the interim committee's stipulations about "academic content." I simply tagged along. We both returned with boxes full of fossils, but I also found twice-a-day walks down the beach useful in the making of poems. William Blake might have seen a world in a grain of sand, but as an English major I could see the metaphoric promise in holding a million years in the palm of my hands each time I picked up a shard of South Carolina mammoth enamel.

The following year we loaded David's mom's Pinto station wagon with camping gear and headed south to the Everglades for a month. Once again it was a biology project that freed us. We wanted to see that million-acre park in Florida. We knew a trip there would take us as close as possible to the Pleistocene without buying a plane ticket to Africa. We rose early with the sun to catch snakes and alligators and to stalk deer. We came close to seeing one of the last Florida panthers, just missing it as it crossed the Flamingo Road in front of a Winnebago we were following. We had no plan in the Everglades. The place was our plan. No tours. No schedule. Cover the park. Walk. Explore.

That was twenty-five years ago. Were those of us who came of age in the sixties and seventies more serious in other less-structured ways than students today? I ask this with a lack of evidence or seriousness. We seemed, in retrospect, so much more open to meandering among "issues," "meaning," and "values." Students today seem more serious in structured ways. I guess I'd say they apply themselves with more focus. Every six years or so there's a pitched battle at the college to do away with the interim. One of the recent compromises has been to add a "graded option" to the courses, and it has proven very popular. It is as if the old "tenured radicals" of the sixties had finally seen enough of the free-flowing stream of experience and want to see the flow controlled by the levy system of grades.

Maybe it's just that there has been a lot of water down the creek of interim since my college years. We've seen "cultural literacy" sweep in and "relevance" swept out. "How will this help my grade point average?" has become the relevant question. We were different, I like to think, and have remained different into our middle age.

Now it's as if my students expect everything timed, tuned, and tamed. Maybe it's what they learn in a childhood of youth-league soccer, dance lessons, and endless peer birthday parties in backyards maintained by lawn services that show up once a week. But then again, maybe it's the whole society. I remember that Reno, Nevada, has a casino that speaks to the *zeitgeist*, a full, fake sky dome that simulates the Nevada heavens over twenty-four hours (the whole cycle compressed to two hours), complete with a roving thunderstorm. When the casino first opened its "sky dome," the storm was programmed to randomly appear on the horizon and move over the tables and slot machines, but the gamblers complained that they wanted the storm to appear "on the hour." The storm was reprogrammed and now people can pause on the hour and watch the "natural" fireworks.

"The extent to which we live from day to day, week to week, intent on details and oblivious to larger presences," Robert Grudin wrote in *Time and the Art of Living*, "is a gauge of our impoverishment in time." When we finally left campus on Monday morning, there were eleven of us in two trucks (one with a trailer full of kayaks) and two SUVs.

We'd decided before leaving that every student would ride with each professor for one stint on the way down. There were plenty of planned stops in the works as we made our way to Hartsville, on Black Creek, and everyone would get a chance to talk with us both. We thought of it as "ice breaking," and the students, we learned later, saw it as a necessary ordeal, like a cold snap of civility, in this warm and fuzzy experience called a "travel interim."

We drove through the South Carolina Piedmont on back roads I knew very well from years of travel. These old routes, laid down by the original travelers, wildlife, and Indians, hug the hills. They follow the contours like bears used to, running the ridges and crossing the gaps between. There are few straight lines as these original highways, not long removed from trails, meander like rivers across the landscape. All my life I've been an adversary of interstates, the way they straighten out a landscape with road cut and in-fill, the way they turn a named place into a number. They take the presence out of place, but they are most likely the future of travel. For most of my students they are the past as well. They are the only travel this generation has known. A twenty-year-old can't imagine driving on back roads for any reason except to empty off the interstates into shopping malls and suburbs. For me and Jim the old landscape is still out there, and it is on a rare day like this one, a day with no schedule to meet, when we can experience place as it best suits us.

"One summer I drove from Spartanburg to Oregon," I said to my passenger of the moment, a sleepy-eyed freshman shuttled into the passenger seat at the last stop. "And not one mile on an interstate highway." She looked at me as if I had just confessed to traveling in a Conestoga wagon.

"Why would you want to do that?" she asked.

"I wanted to feel it," I laughed. "The distances and the bigness of this country."

"Didn't it take forever?"

"Maybe three or four days longer," I said. "That's not much time in the depths of a whole summer."

"That's one long road trip, Professor Lane."

—

My true education began with a college geology teacher, John Harrington, who died in 1986 at the age of sixty-nine. I learned at least three good things from him: to read the land and discover in the dance of imagination and reason an intelligible world; to slide ideas against one another like sticks and delight in the sparks and smoke; and to see the connections that can be made in the world around me.

Harrington gave me a world where time moves in more than one direction and no landscape holds steady for long. Because of him I see children slide off benches the way glaciers slide down a mountain. I see lakes where they no longer exist and connections between grain sales and the paleoclimate of Russia.

In 1986, three weeks before his death from cancer, I had visited Harrington to confirm again the magic of his teaching. I had been a student of his in the midseventies and an occasional correspondent since graduation. He was Wofford College's resident professor emeritus but had been confined to his bedroom since January. We could not walk the soapstone ridge near Lawson's Fork Creek as we had done many times in the past. The landscape of words and ideas would have to be a fitting field trip.

As we sat in his house on the outskirts of Spartanburg, he tried to convince me that he "was no Svengali." The magic he had worked for twenty years teaching geology at Wofford was nothing more than "having a little fun with rocks," he insisted. Harrington claimed he was just following in the field clothes of a few teachers who had taught him to have a little fun. "Just passing on a little understanding," he said.

When fresh out of graduate school Harrington briefly worked for an oil company, but he found out in the first six months that he wasn't a corporate man. That's when he accepted a teaching post at

SMU. He taught the course designed to get rid of people who could not make it as geologists. He lasted seven years.

By the end, in 1955, he was spreading himself too thin: heading up his department, overseeing a consulting firm downtown, teaching classes, writing papers for geology journals. He also had trouble, as he put it, "being a lion tamer."

"The lion tamer doesn't actually tame anything," Harrington had said back then. "He gets in there with a chair and a whip and a gun but really only stays within the genetic boundaries the cats have established. As a teacher I felt the same way. I wasn't changing any of them. They were jumping on chairs because they knew it was safer there."

That year, while reading Rudyard Kipling's *Just So Stories* to his daughter, Harrington made a discovery that would change his life and teaching: "I realized I wasn't teaching students anything if they couldn't answer Kipling's 'why,' 'how,' and 'which' questions." His students at SMU wanted to be taught "to be good technicians" so that they could get jobs with oil companies. They did not see education as something they needed; graduation was what they needed. When Harrington tried to start teaching in a new way—a way he was not prepared for himself—he had a virtual riot on his hands.

A group of young geologists—one now a famous geologist with the space program—went to the dean and claimed that Harrington was incompetent. Their teacher gave the class a chance to vote on his methods. The students voted twenty-eight to two, with one abstaining vote, to uphold the charge of incompetence. Harrington admitted that from the students' standpoint they were right. He resigned from the university in the summer of 1956. "You don't always succeed," he said.

In his last book, *Dance of the Continents,* Harrington described insight as the art of becoming personally aware. The insights of those Wednesday geology labs—in which Harrington taught me to see—are imprinted on my mind as clearly as the formula for the molecular structure of water, the multiplication tables, or the parts of speech. In conversation Harrington talked a great deal about genius. He suggested that genius was a field where anyone can stand. It was not some holy city populated only by people with high SAT scores or gifted and talented credentials or top-of-the-scale grade point averages.

One of the quickest ways to gain insight for Harrington was to open the door of time. He was once collecting rocks on the cliffs at Lyme Regis on the southern coast of England. There he found an ancient ax head, a relic of paleo-Britain preserved among the cliff's rocks. Harrington then imagined the human being who made the ax so clearly that he was transported in time. "Separation in time was all that kept us from sharing my peanuts," he said about the moment.

His genius may have been his pestering mind. No one was safe from the questions. Not college deans nor freshmen nor fellow travelers on airplanes and buses. When he got the answers, he let reason—what he called "least astonishment"—put them into context. "Follow me," Harrington told the class I was in. We boarded buses, and he took us to see the world.

"I'm weak as water," Harrington said the last time I saw him. I thought of rivers taking down mountains. As a teacher, I've begun to ask Kipling's—and Harrington's—questions of my students. As he taught me, I work daily to see life—and death—in context. Einstein once noted that "the example of the great and pure individual is the only thing that can lead us to noble thoughts and deeds." John Harrington hunted the pure paths of genius for much of his life. And in addition, he convinced a significant number more that they too can follow that path and discover genius in the context of every glistening stone.

———

It was only when Jim and I read the student journals after our return that we understood how much the students hated the trip down. The "time thing" really did them in. Though no one waited for us at our Hartsville destination and there was no schedule beyond our own meandering exploration, the students found it maddening to have no real sense where we were "headed." We were rolling "downstate," and that was enough for me but not for them.

After a week of talking about "watershed thinking," a concept that landscapes can be reorganized by drainage patterns rather than political and engineering decisions, I thought we had them prepared. That Monday we left Spartanburg (within view of the Blue Ridge, the headwaters of many Piedmont streams) and drove slowly southeast on old South Carolina Highway 9, crossed the Lawson's Fork watershed, the Pacolet, the Broad, the Catawba, the Lynches, until we finally slipped almost unnoticed at Pageland into the drainage of the Pee Dee and our study stream, Black Creek. As I imagined the trip, we would lose almost seven hundred feet in altitude and pass from the hilly Piedmont of red clay and hardwoods into the pine-studded sand hills. What was exciting about interim was that there would be time to pass through half the state as we drove down. We could take the whole day and experience at least two distinct landscapes. I had said all this in class the morning before we prepared to leave.

But saying something is not enough to make a difference. The student experience: "How could a two-hour trip be turned into one lasting seven hours?" one asked in her journal. "Here's how: stay off the interstates and stop for every possible distraction along the way." I'll admit that the trip probably wouldn't have gone by the syllabus, even if there had been one. I had planned to stop at the Broad River and point out the long, rocky shoal, the most significant deterrent to river travel between the upstate and low country early in the nineteenth century, but by the time we found a pull-off, we were well up the hill from the river. When I started my tale of canals, locks, and commerce, I saw that very few of the students had even noticed we had crossed the Broad. So we pushed on further east—to the distractions of a well-preserved lock system on the Catawba River at Landsford Canal State Park. Here the students wandered the old footpath and looked confused as to how this had anything to do with Black Creek.

I wanted them to see context: how the Piedmont province is a reality we were moving over—rocky underbelly exposed in "nick points" in rivers, which caused their forefathers great concern because they slowed commerce, similar to the consternation the students were feeling for being isolated from their interstate bubble. "They feel a need for speed," I said to Jim when we stopped once, quoting *Top Gun*. "I find all I want to do is slow down, more and more."

"I don't want a moccasin kit," Jim added at lunch when I told him the students were getting edgy at so much stopping. "You remember when you went to camp and headed straight to the craft shop and they sold you the kit. In it was everything you needed—a stamped-out leather shoe, rawhide string to stitch it together, directions. You got the whole thing and they told you exactly how it would fit."

And so we pushed on. By the time we arrived on the outskirts of Pageland, one of the later stops in the day, the students were crazy for direction. In contrast, my heart was pumping with the anticipation of reaching the headwaters of Black Creek. Soon we had crossed the tiny town's city limits and I knew we were ripening toward my goal for the day. I could feel it. Behind us was the red clay Piedmont. A few dozen miles below us was the coastal plain; thick, black loam; alluvial bottomland; sand ridges. The headwaters of Black Creek were nearby. "A kind of expectation, based on obvious metaphors, attaches to sources and headwaters," Franklin Burroughs writes in *The River Home*, one of our textbooks. Burroughs's book is a long, meandering trip down the Waccamaw River, two watersheds east of our study area, and when we had discussed the literary journey the week before leaving, the students had difficulty with the pace just as they had struggled all day with our route.

Jim was leading as we entered Pageland and, I must admit, the search for the headwaters of Black Creek was not a precision act. Jim had a topo map and was navigating by its special magic, a magic that was new to him. I knew Jim did not have a town map, so he had to follow landscape features and roads without names. Twice he turned down the wrong roads and we caravaned a mile or so in the general direction of the creek, then three-point-turned back in the other direction. When I passed the two SUVs, the students looked dumbstruck, confused. Through the windows I could tell it was not their quest for the holy grail. It was a wild goose chase. When Jim finally turned next to a cemetery, I knew that he had his bearings. I remembered the landmark from studying the map before we left Spartanburg. This "pointless circling" around in a tiny Piedmont town was another such "distraction" for the students.

As I followed Jim's truck, I considered the headwaters stop, as if it were the answer to some mystery. Headwaters. The Source. These are words shot through with symbolism. I had pulled out the topo maps at home countless times before we left for our trip. I had read the elevation and contour lines like a code. Now I was within a mile of the source.

When we pulled all the vehicles over on a shoulderless tar road on the backside of that little South Carolina village, I was crazy with anticipation and I was not disappointed. I stepped out of the truck and looked west and east. West of the road was one of the source streams, a clear spring running fast down from a nearby coppice of trees. To the east, below the road, was a farm pond silting in with age. A great blue heron lifted from the backside of the pond as we stopped. "This is it," I said to my student passenger. "This is the beginning of Black Creek's mysterious meander through two geographic provinces to the Pee Dee and on to the sea."

The students noted the moment in their journals. Some of them had even fallen under the spell of origins, if not time. One had seen my excitement and noted, "I realized his love for water and how intrigued he is with the whole idea of watershed thinking." She went on to reflect, "After I thought about it, I realized that this was partly the beginning of our two-week study. His eagerness and excitement rubbed off on me as I discovered this was where it all began."

Where what began? That is the question that intrigues me now. This headwaters stop was but one moment in a long series for my students. Was it learning? Was it experience? Maybe one of them will become a writer like me or a finance professor sometime returning to a home landscape. I'm beginning to understand now that it's not the content of interims that matters. It's their form. We form and flow from headwater moments.

After everyone posed for what Jim would come to call a "sorority photo moment" (seven girls with their faces pressed together), we piled back in the vehicles, the last of the students stuck with me. As we left the headwaters behind, it occurred to me: this is the future of "higher" education—tiny floating moments of insight in a flood of pressure, stress, expectation, and obligation. "A teacher affects eternity," says a clear paperweight on Jim's desk at Wofford. As we drove toward Hartsville, I looked for eternity in the face of my new sidekick, a freshman bent on the next destination and getting there in decent time.

Death

by

Water

In the first dream I remember, I'm running down a drainage ditch (I was maybe five at the time) followed by a rising wall of rushing water ready to overwhelm me. We were living in Southern Pines, North Carolina. It was the year my father committed suicide, so the dream might be easily explained in terms of personal apocalypse, but it's the water I focus on when I remember it. Water can be so many things—source, purifying agent, flux, infusion, salvation ("water of life"), and grave. Jesus walked on the water, and the Buddha in his assumption sermon saw a mountain lake (with clear water, sand, shells, snails, and fishes) like a path to redemption.

Wordsworth, in the sixth section of *The Prelude,* calls a whitewater river he's walking along in the Alps "tumult and peace, the darkness and the light." Water is an aspect of my interior landscape to which I often return, and it remains central to my understanding of the world as a roaring river.

"There is an opening downward within each moment," James Hillman says early in *The Dream and the Underworld,* "an unconscious reverberation." I am a kayaker, and I know nothing loves down more than a river. Hillman says later, in "Praxis," a section about dream images, that there are at least five rivers associated with Hades: "the frigid Styx; the burning Pyriphlegethon; the mournful, wailing Cocytus; the depressive, black Acheron; and Lethe," the stream of "Remembering and Forgetting." If there is topography in Hades, as Hillman argues, then there must be whole watersheds below. Hillman fails to mention whether any of these Hades rivers have significant stretches of white water, but I would bet the Lethe, in its upper reaches, falls through some heavy gradient.

Entering water, Hillman says, "relaxes one's hold on things and lets go of where one has been stuck." To enter too deeply into water for a kayaker is Hades. That's why we learn the Eskimo roll, to keep from staying down for too long. We know too well what Hillman knows, that moving water, like soul itself, has within it a special relationship to death. Ocean. Lake. River. They all rage and they all can kill. Call it physics, or try to explain it away through luck and hydrology, but if people associate with moving water long enough, tragedy will come.

I was paddling the Big Laurel Creek on a summer day in 1989 when I learned my lesson about the tragedy moving water can conjure. After ten years of paddling I had achieved a degree of mastery of the kayak. I lived in a paddling community and boated with other people of similar skills. We felt capable and assured of every move. Hades had not yet touched me.

It was a difficult, isolated run through a beautiful Appalachian creek gorge. I remember the water was high, but we had a perfect run. We were all advanced paddlers (I think there were four of us), and so each rapid was a challenge but not the real nightmare factory white water can be if someone in the group is unprepared for the difficulty. One of the people I was paddling with was Bunny Johns, then vice president of the Nantahala Outdoor Center.

The Big Laurel empties into the French Broad just above Frank Bell Rapid, the last significant drop on that stretch of river. Our takeout that afternoon was the NOC French Broad Outpost. After we had paddled through the last rapid, a river-wide ledge called Surprise, we eddied out in front of the outpost. A guide was waiting for Bunny. Soon she was on the phone, already privy to a tragedy unfolding on the Tuckaseegee, a river close to the NOC's main outpost in Wesser and a river often used for beginning kayak clinics.

We quickly lashed on our kayaks, packed our gear, and drove back toward Wesser; Bunny filled us in on what had transpired on the Tuckaseegee. The day had started normal enough with the routine beginners kayak clinic, but in the first hour on the river things turned terrible quickly. The clinic leader, a very experienced instructor, had led the excited novice paddlers through a simple class II rapid near the top of the river; though slightly bold from high rains, there should have been nothing dangerous on this river. As best as Bunny could figure from limited information, one student, Roger Stallings, a man in his early thirties, had somehow tangled his boat in something obstructing the river and quickly drowned. His body had not been recovered, so there was no chance to revive him.

It turned out later that the junk was an industrial conveyer belt probably washed out of a landfill upstream by the high water. The long, stiff, abrasive belt had been lodged between two rocks, invisible, pulsing to the surface in a standing wave in the middle of the rapid.

The belt (we saw later, watching from the shore) would appear every three or four minutes. Stallings was the unlucky one to intersect his kayak with it. His plastic boat folded around his legs and he was drowned. The boat, his life jacket, and his spray jacket all washed up, but his body disappeared, swirling down into the muddy, rain-thickened river. I had paddled the same river that week and run the exact route, so it could just as easily have been me or the instructor or any one of several dozen boaters who probably ran the river that week.

The rescue squad was there when we arrived about two hours after the drowning. Bunny gathered what information she could at riverside and then departed for the main outpost to begin contacting Stallings's family and organizing the company for the search and investigation into what exactly had happened on the Tuckaseegee that morning.

I understood the odds of the situation. The drowning was an event as rare as a one-hundred-year flood. NOC is considered one of the most professional outfitters in the world, renowned for its safety precautions and technical training of clinic participants. There was never, from the beginning, any suggestion that the guide or the Outdoor Center had been negligent. "The Harvard of white water instruction," the clinic program had once been called by *Outside* magazine. The blame could be placed nowhere. The water had worked its dark logic with an unsuspecting kayaker.

I was still dressed to paddle, so right away I drove to the put-in with a group of NOC guides who had brought a raft. A half mile upstream we launched the raft and paddled quickly downstream and did all we could do; we began to look for the body. Payson Kennedy, the president of the company, was in the raft, and he pulled us along with strong strokes in the boat's bow. I remember the silence as we floated down that short stretch of the Tuckaseegee in the raft. Usually rafting is carefree, but this short trip had the smell of death and tragedy hanging all about it.

We swung the raft back and forth across the rapid (several guides had already set up safety ropes to ferry us back and forth through the swift current) and probed with long sticks for the body. We did this for hours the first day with no success.

I returned every day after work (I worked at the NOC store at that time) and continued to ride in the raft, to probe the river bottom with a long pole. One day the rescue squad brought in a diver, and he paddled back and forth in deep eddies like a trout, looking for some sign of Stallings's body. On shore the scene took on the feel of a Southern wake as restaurants brought food for the rescue squad and us. The hoods of trucks were spread with biscuits, hamburgers, ham, and deviled eggs. There were urns of sweet tea set up in the shade, and we drank deeply from them on our breaks.

Day after day we did not find him. The rescue workers assured me the corpse would "float up," probably a week into the process when the natural chemistry of necrology countered the natural cooling of the river. One day family members showed up at the site of the drowning. It was an awkward and terrible time, and I prayed that we would not find the body that day, that he would be recovered among strangers instead.

Each morning that week we sent out two kayakers to paddle slowly the six miles downstream to Bryson City, scouting the bank for the missing body. When word came six days into the search that the kayakers had spotted the body, we jumped into a raft and stroked the three miles downstream. We ran all the rapids in silence, a floating ambulance or a hearse bound for the scene of an accident. After a half hour we saw the two kayakers standing on a small beach on the left bank of the river, looking awkward in their gear. The rescue squad had worked down to the river on the right bank. Stallings's brother-in-law was waiting as well. They all stood helpless to recover the body. What separated them was twenty yards of swift current. They needed our raft to ferry them across so that they could retrieve the body.

We grounded the raft on the small beach. I glanced at the snag. I could see Roger Stallings's body resting in the branches of a tall tree that blocked a left bend of the river. I had been told that the dead look very dead, but I was not prepared for what I saw. I could see the top of his head and his black hair flowing peacefully in the current. I could see the top of his right shoulder where the river had stripped it of clothing. It was ghostly white. There was no smell.

Two guides from NOC ferried the coroner across in a canoe. He had to declare the kayaker dead before the work could begin to recover the body. We waited in the raft as a canoe came across with the coroner.

As soon as the coroner had done his work, he jumped in the raft and we pointed it into the current and ferried across to where the rescue squad stood waiting. Two of the squad members were dressed in yellow suits with rubber gloves and wore masks over their mouths. They tossed a black body bag into the raft. I could see the silver grommets that would allow the river water to drain out freely. The dead kayaker's brother-in-law climbed in the raft with the men in the yellow suits. They settled in and we ferried in reverse, back to the small beach. The two rescue squad members climbed out and waded into the current to recover the body.

In a vivid dream I remember from around the time of the drowning, I'm driving past a flooding river. I get out and look down into the colliding current. It's obvious I can't paddle such difficult surging water, but just as I'm ready to leave, a single kayaker starts down with great skill and caution. When I look close, I realize it's me. In the dream I know now that I am riding one of the rivers of Hades.

That moment on the Tuckaseegee was James Hillman's "opening downward"; it was when I was swallowed up by Hades the first time. It was when I stopped being a kayaker in some significant way. Simply put, one kayaker in me died and another was born. In some deeper way that was the first time I came to terms with what Hillman calls "the subtle kinds of death." The physical death of Roger Stallings affected me deeply, but it was the tiny deaths within myself that set me to different purposes.

The two rescue squad members made the recovery quickly and efficiently. They untangled the dead kayaker from the tree; slipped his body into the bag; zipped up the heavy, black zipper; and floated their burden to the beach. His shoulder and the top of his head was really all I ever saw of him. The nightmare week finally came to an end when we grabbed a corner of the bag and hefted it into the middle of the raft. The Tuckaseegee was my own river Styx. The men in yellow climbed in. We nosed the black rubber raft into the current a second time, experienced boatmen keeping our steady line across the river, swinging us all—living and dead—efficiently to the other shore.

Four

FAMILY

WILDERNESS

Think of those old, enduring
   connections
found in all flesh—the
   channeling
wires and threads, vacuoles,
   granules,
plasma and pods, purple veins,
   ascending
boles and coral sapwood (sugar-
and light-filled), those
   common
   ligaments,
filaments, fibers and canals.
—Pattiann Rogers,
"The Family Is All There Is"

One

Family

Line

On the top of my great-great-grandfather John Lane's limestone grave marker in eastern North Carolina there is a set of carved hands grasped in friendship. The marker was erected in 1868. Who is this patriarchal John Lane shaking hands with? God? If I think of my paternal family line extending toward the present, John Lane is shaking hands with his son George Washington, who in turn shakes hands with his son Robert Preston, who in turn shakes hands with his son, John Edward, who in due time takes my tiny infant hand at my birth in 1954.

It's a good line, though a short one. Five men standing side by side. A genealogist friend has one of his family lines traced back to three kings of England, another line back to Charlemagne. Like me, he is childless, but he's still hoping. He dates young women approaching thirty who still have the certainty of family written all over them like an alphabet.

I was once briefly married, and I've disappointed the family dreams of more than a few young women, but unlike my friend the genealogist I've instead fallen in love with the idea that my family history is a story, and I am at the end of it. In the story I am not some minor character wandering the middle acts where things get complicated, waiting for the king to show. I am a climax of sorts. I am a writer, a scratcher of crooked lines. Instead of a child, I leave a lasting legacy of paper, a canceled check on my branch of the bank of Lane.

I am also an inept historian and a poor genealogist, sloppy with the facts. I sometimes make mistakes recording names and dates and jump to conclusions based on too little information. I get bored quickly in official archives. Instead of accepting the blessed assurance that raw data gives a good historian or genealogist, I doodle on the corners of my notepads while I should be recording long successions of rare tax records only available to me in state libraries. I should look for provable nuance and lead, but when given a choice between certainty and speculation, I follow speculation's lead the way Hansel and Gretel followed bread crumbs. Even with my short line, the family the writer in me invents is more interesting than the one filed safely away in the creases of historic record.

When I wander down my father's family line, the sensation is overwhelming that I am headed not out of the dark forest toward certainty and safety, but instead I'm headed deeper into uncertainty. Writers find comfort in the murky provisions the unknown has provided unasked for.

Meditation always pulls me back to Greene County, North Carolina, where my father's blood is pooled. The drainage is slow there. People, like water, tend to creep along, occasionally catch in a depression, and turn dark with one stain or another. Greene County is flat, coastal country tending gradually toward the Atlantic, less than one hundred miles away. "That's the middle of nowhere," a friend once said when I pointed out on a road map where my father's family is from.

Greene County is perfect land for farming, which is all my father's line has done there for two centuries. Farming is an occupation that makes deep impact on the land, but most farmers don't leave much of a trail except for deeds, wills, and on the larger plantations, ledger books. You could take all the papers I've found directly associated with my line's five generations in Greene County and not fill up a medium lockbox in my local bank.

Maybe the paper trail is there, though. I have never followed the research checklist given me by one of my serious, careful genealogist friends: I haven't located the family Bible yet; there are family letters left unread; I've only done a few interviews; I've never visited the Greene County courthouse and sorted through birth certificates, marriage records, wills, estates, deeds, mortgages; I've only tracked down a few cemetery records, county histories, tax lists, newspaper articles, voter records; I've spent one weekend in the North Carolina state archives looking for the land grant, census, and militia records, but I haven't been back.

When I thumb through my notebook, it is not the absences that bother me—the missing names, dates, and marriages; it is not the hope for more information stringing me deeper into the past that stalls me, brooding over family. Instead I'm overwhelmed by what I do have, by the presences already known to me.

When I look back over the traceable line—almost two hundred years of Lane family history—I see great-great-grandfather John (1802–68) and his six children; great-grandfather George Washington (1828–1907) with his seven; grandfather Robert Preston (1871–1963) with eleven; and my father, John (1915–59), with only me (b. 1954). A meditation on this legacy is like looking at the complex syntax of a Faulknerian sentence, each generation a complex clause, and then realizing that I am the period.

—

If I prove to be that period, maybe my father can be seen as the verb. The action word. The motivating premise. My father comes to me from four sources: pictures, a few personal effects, stories from people who knew him, and my own stifled memory. My father, as he comes back to me, is still full of surprises, both minefield and garden. It wasn't until I was in my twenties, going through my father's old wallet one day, that I realized my father was five-six. I am six-two. Minefield or garden?

I had a picture of my father displayed over my desk at college. He was smiling. It was a head-and-shoulder shot, and he was wearing a field jacket and a helmet liner. It was taken somewhere in Europe during the Second World War. 1942 or '43. The liner sits at an angle, and a shadow falls like a woolen hat across his upper forehead.

One day I noticed something as simple as my father's teeth. They were sharp and a little crooked, not at all like my own. I searched the surface of the photograph for some clue to his suicide, his past, and the way his life would exert itself upon the flow of my own. What would my father look like with a beard, one like his son had worn since his first years of college?

One day I went through a shoe box where for years I'd stored a few of my father's things, mostly war souvenirs. I unfolded a map my father had brought back from the war. There were eight names written around the edge of a sketch of Sicily. The names were written in faded, forty-year-old ink, each in the hand of a stranger who was in the engineers with him: men from Waycross, Georgia; Valhalla, New York.

I tried to call the men who had signed it. I chose a name at random. Michael Cohen from Valhalla. I called directory assistance for New York and asked for Valhalla, and then I asked for Michael Cohen.

"We don't have a Michael Cohen in Valhalla."

My heart drifted down. Of course they would not. It had been forty years. There was a silent moment.

"But we do have a Michael Cohen in Russet, a village nearby."

I took down the number and called.

"Yes, this is Michael Cohen. Yes, I was in the First Army in World War II. No, no I don't remember anyone by that name."

Then the voice on the other end warmed up a little and began to talk more openly. He had been a lieutenant in the engineering unit. They had seen action in every major European campaign—North Africa, Sicily, Italy, Normandy, the Battle of the Bulge—and they had been discharged in Czechoslovakia at the end of the war. I knew that my father had been an enlisted man. I read Mr. Cohen the rest of the names. There was one he recognized, the boy from Waycross, Georgia.

"He was one hell of a poker player. I lost a bunch of my pay to him. And there was another Southern boy who was his friend. He was a good player too. Those Southern boys were good at cards."

I listed the rest of the names but made no other connections.

I showed the map to my mother. I explained about the war and Sicily. My mother shook her head.

"I can't imagine your father asking those men to sign," my mother had said, looking at the map. "He must have been tight."

My mother often says that when she met my father in 1947, he was always tight, drinking a quart of whiskey a day. He worked his job at the service station in spite of his drinking. His brothers have told me that no one ever remembers seeing him unable to function because of drinking.

"How can a man drink a quart of whiskey a day?" I asked an alcoholic once.

"It's easy. You get up in the morning and you bubble about eight ounces," he explained. "And then you sneak off midmorning and you bubble about five more. Then at lunch you bubble eight more and then midafternoon some more. When your shift's over, you can go home and start the serious drinking until you pass out."

The last time I was in Greene County, I went looking for my father's grave. My grandfather Robert Preston Lane is buried in the same cemetery. I found my grandfather's grave with no problem, safe among a clan of Lanes—cousins, brothers, my grandmother. At first I couldn't locate the flat, military service marker that had served to note my father's place in the Lane plot since his suicide in 1959. I remembered him being buried in a solitary plot on the town side of the cemetery, and a cousin who was with me remembered the plot being farther toward the woods.

We finally found him near the trees. It was the third or fourth time as an adult I had visited my father's grave. I thought of the strange drifting line that would trail behind me over the landscape of Greene County if I were to walk from my father's grave to my grandfather's grave in the same cemetery, then hike three miles down the county road to the small family cemetery where my great-grandfather and great-great-grandfather are buried. Four graves, not really in a line. The line was only in my imagination.

"The past is not dead. Sometimes it isn't even past," Faulkner said. Faulkner knew we don't stand in a line. It's more like a circle, and anyone at anytime can be the center. Family stories make the sentence of our lives present tense.

When someone asks me directly why I've not committed to extending the family line, I often avoid the question with an answer of another sort: "I'm leaving behind six or seven cubic feet of paper—published and unpublished books, letters, manuscripts, journals—in an archive somewhere. That will be my only claim on history."

Occasionally, when intimacy has softened the edges of a conversation, I'll offer a more complex answer, an explanation approaching confession: family fear has kept me childless—the fear of failing as a father, the fear of commitment, the fear that I would abandon a child or fail to provide, much as my father did.

My commitment has fallen to craft, to career. I have file cabinets full of letters and manuscripts and a personal journal now stretching back twenty years. I understand that many people have marriage, children. They follow as natural as rain. But I have made a choice: silence, space, and imagination over noise, clutter, and reality. Growing anything takes care and time, and I've always figured if I was to put the time and care into growing children, then what would happen to my prose, my sheaf of poems, my reading room, my publication shelf? Some would call it the most selfish of choices.

But it is my choice. A friend claims it is a peculiar male thing to think of one's accomplishments in lengths—a short shelf of publications in my case—but that doesn't stop me. I walk into my living room from time to time and glance at my publication shelf the way a father checks a sleeping child.

Last Christmas I began to photocopy the first ten years of my journal, handwritten in a variety of spiral notebooks and bound books. I wanted two copies in case of fire. This Christmas I plan to take on the daunting task of photocopying the most recent ten years, a period of long-winded reflection, speculation, and quotidian accounting. The accumulated journal could run to twenty thousand photocopied pages. I've never completely understood why I write in a journal. Sometimes a poem will emerge, or a fragment of a story, but not often. I don't read back through the pages with deep interest or regularity either, but the journal grows like an embryo within the body of my daily experience.

Fifteen years ago, before I had a house of my own (or a publication shelf), I was in the attic of my mother's house sorting through my already growing archive of paper. My sister, Sandy, was there with me. Sandy is a woman who mistrusts paper clutter and clears her house of the accumulation of it once a year. She shook her head and smiled as I ordered and filed personal letters, carbons of my responses, and unpublished manuscripts. "What makes you so sure anyone will care that you kept all this?" she asked.

I didn't know what to say. I could answer her now: I knew, even then, that someone would care because I care. There will always be people like me who search the scraps of the past for insights into the present and future.

Even then, when my sister asked the question, I knew that I wasn't assuring the world that I "mattered" as much as I was confirming that reflection matters, craft matters, writing matters. I believe my need for that six cubic feet of paper in some archive is a creature need, as strong and healthy as the drive for family. With each layer of drafts, letters, and journals I am like a desert pack rat adding my layer of confirming refuse to the human nest.

I knew from early on that it was not a question of greatness or fame; if not famous, I would at least be obsessively documented. Few people commit to such a task: keep every letter, draft, and rejection slip. "Live in the layers," Stanley Kunitz has said.

———

My father's family line is one of farmers, not writers. My Aunt Eula was the one I knew best among my father's siblings. She was neither farmer nor writer. Her kingdom was the small, Southern town, the present, the gossip of Greene Street, and the news of nearby cousins. I spent every summer after my father's suicide with Aunt Eula in Snow Hill, the county seat of Greene County. It was a childhood of sweet corn and tobacco barns. In the 1960s it was an agricultural present soon to be past.

Aunt Eula did write a few short letters on pink stationery that kept me informed about my father's family. She sent money too, ten or twenty dollars for Christmas or my birthday. When I visited the family farms, she saw to it that my uncles told stories to fill the missing pages on my father, how he had driven a school bus to be his own man, how he'd been the first from the county to enlist in the army. I listened and remembered.

In 1988, a few summers before Aunt Eula died, I was visiting her, reading in her sunny den. I saw a reference to a "Lane House" in a history of Greene County. My Aunt Eula had never mentioned the existence of this abandoned plantation house or the family graveyard under the huge sycamore that the book described.

"What about this big house?" I asked Aunt Eula. "It says it's the oldest house in the county."

"That's the old Lane place," she answered.

"What old Lane place? I thought the place where you and Daddy were born was the old Lane place."

"No, that place was built by my granddaddy, G. W. Lane. *That's* the old Lane place," she said, pointing toward the picture. "It's in the Jones tobacco field. The old Lane cemetery is there," she said matter-of-factly.

That May afternoon, in a pouring rain shower, we drove up a long drive into the middle of a tobacco field and explored my ancestral home for the first and only time. My mother and aunt sat in the car, uninterested in the house. I went into the house with my sister, Sandy, and took pictures, walked around. The fireplaces were intact. The old doors were still in their door frames. No one had stolen the original mantels. Someone had scrawled "Race Masters" with spray paint on the old, plaster walls. Upstairs, the house had closets, what seemed a rarity in the eighteenth or nineteenth century.

Hay had been stored in the downstairs rooms, but the floors were still solid and some of the original windows were still in the panes. The house was well preserved, and the Greene County history dated it as "mid–Seventeen hundreds"; we would find out later from Mr. Vernon Jones, whose family owned it, that nobody had lived there for forty years. It had been over a hundred years, I would find out later, since a Lane had lived there.

It was still pouring rain when my sister and I left the family house. Though it was late, I was pulled toward the cemetery. There were the remains of an old fence, and some of the stones had fallen from lack of care. "I want to see what those stones at the center say," I told my sister.

The heart of the family cemetery was domed by the new growth from a snarl of blackberry canes. I pushed them aside with a broken tobacco stick and saw two stones: John Lane, dead in 1868, and Mary Lane, 1865. I was stunned. There was my name—and the name of my mother. I went back to the car and pulled out paper and pencil as my mother and aunt waited, uninterested in what we had discovered. My sister helped me work through the cemetery in the rain, and I sketched the layout of every standing stone.

They say the Mormons store their genealogical records in a deep cave in the Utah desert. When I visit family cemeteries, I daydream of visiting that cave and riding the elevator deep into reamed-out bedrock to see a million names with birth and death dates, the ones the Mormons have secretly carved in stone to preserve, to assure their survival.

It is survival I want most in life, for someone to say, a hundred, two hundred years from now, "That was his life. That's the way he lived back then." Forty years separate me from my father's tragic death, and yet I'm still walking cemeteries searching.

When Aunt Eula died in 1992, we cleaned out her house. What I was looking for was letters, a cache of letters from my father. But Aunt Eula was a woman like my sister. You could never call her a pack rat. Her house was clear of the past. Her mail was answered, then thrown away.

In our culture a direct line of descent runs through the fathers. The family name is the father's name. The genealogy tables are ordered this way; a "family tree" it's called, and the men are definitely the trunk. The names of fathers, sons, grandfathers, great-grandfathers make for a thick shade.

Women, such as Aunt Eula—childless herself—are always to the left or right of the direct line, peopling a family, but not extending it. A line continues from father to son, from family name to family name. The daughters marry and continue someone else's line. But it is only through the women that true descent can be traced, descent in the scientific sense. Nuclear DNA, that passed on by both fathers and mothers, cannot be traced from generation to generation—it divides and divides and divides like a farm carved up in wills—but mitochondrial DNA is passed on from mother to mother whole. The father's nuclear DNA does not interest scientists when trying to solve a family mystery dating back several generations. It's a gamble, not a sure thing.

In 1997, as the June heat was beginning to build, I arrived in Wilson, North Carolina, for a visit with my father's eighty-three-year-old first cousin Jenny. The winter before my visit, Jenny had written me a note (now filed away in my cabinet) saying, "All the old ones are gone. They've even torn down the old house. Come to see me."

Jenny is spry. She remembers things and articulates them. Several months before my arrival she had moved from her family house on Kincaid Street where she had lived for seventy-three years. The house was built by her father, my grandfather's brother Zebalon Baynard Lane, on the outskirts of Wilson, a farming center in the county next to Greene. The city has overtaken the country around it, and even Jenny has left central Wilson for a condominium in a local retirement village on the present sprawling outskirts that could be anywhere. Jenny told us how she had sold her house and how a young couple had remodeled it already. Soon it would be forgotten as a "Lane house," she worried.

Jenny's living room is full of family heirlooms. "This was your great-great-aunt Angeline's melodeon," Jenny said, leaning lightly against the small piano, the keys covered by a dark, mahogany panel.

Jenny told me about my father. She and my father had been born less than a month apart in 1915, and she remembered him being "melancholy," even as a boy. Jenny complained that her grasp of words was fading; she complained as someone would who had taught English and spent her life among books. But this time she had the perfect word, and she repeated it: "melancholy." I liked her use of that word, like something out of the world of the romantic poets. My father, the melancholic. It placed him for me in a huge, spiraling family of Lanes that I've always had trouble keeping straight.

Jenny then drew out a file folder. In with the family papers Jenny had John Lane and G. W. Lane's original wills, encased in plastic. She pulled them out and placed them on the dining room table. "Read them out loud," my cousin Jenny said. John Lane had set his last will and testament down on the eighth day of August 1868. He was "somewhat feeble in health but of sound disposing mind and memory," and his will was witnessed by his two sons, George and Joseph. His three daughters were well provided for; he left them over four hundred acres of land and the big house and "desires it that if either of my above named daughters shall mary [sic] and leave other two single that the married one Shall not draw the house and lot when in the dwelling stands so that it may remain a home for the two single ones." Where I could not read the words, where the paper was torn or the ink faded or the nineteenth century handwriting obscure, I filled in the gaps.

Cousin Jenny told me that the big house had been torn down. "Sold to a furniture maker in Scotland Neck," Jenny said as we looked at the two old wills and talked about our line's past.

Jenny had paid the furniture maker to craft a small bookshelf from pine boards pulled from the flooring of the old house. She brought it out for me to see. I felt sad and full of grief. The shelf had a small, gold plaque with the words "The Lane House" engraved in script. The shelf was such a diminishment of the house, merely a sanded fragment of the two-hundred-year-old dwelling, the old nails clipped clean, the heart-pine grain swirling like flame through the varnished surface.

She had the man's number, and I told her I wanted to make a bed from the old beams. Jenny encouraged me to call, handed me the phone.

When I called, the furniture maker cleared up some things for me about the old house: yes, the unusual closets in the house were original, a rarity in houses of its age; the floor joists had powder post beetles in them, but the beams in the ceiling were thirty-eight feet long. The age of the house? "There were no handmade nails, so the house was built between the 1790s and the late teens."

"Could you make me a bed?" I asked.

"I'll send you some plans. The wood has been put to good use," he said. "The handrail from the entry hall went to a beautiful house in Wilson in eight pieces."

When the man had finished salvaging what wood he could use, he piled the rest with a front-end loader and burned it.

—

Isn't it enough to walk in an old, family house, to discover a family cemetery, to see back over one hundred years to a namesake's handwriting, to catch one's name meandering toward the present from the past in the stories of an old cousin, to have a bed made from salvaged beams? I have never believed so; I would answer no, it isn't enough. There should be someone around to write it down. Too many clues are to be found "in the archives" and reasoned into a story to stop at visits, conversations, present experiences.

But the living mistrust paper trails and the dead have nothing to say about it. Whom do we honor? I think we honor the dead, and maybe writing is their realm. "Remember me," the ghost of Hamlet's father says. When I took my first teaching job, the English Department chair walked me around the campus and said, "If I have any advice for you, it is that you can say anything you want to any-body here, but never write anything down." I'm the end of a line, and to give up writing all this down would be to give up on the past.

I am not a farmer of facts or land. I am not what one of my gay friends calls "a breeder boy." Though heterosexual, I have no children, no progeny. My genetic bank account is closed, and I barter script for my place in the line. Call it choice; call it a deep wound; call it a family fear wide as the Cape Fear River. Probably there will be no direct descendant figuring out the same information I lose my way in—who begat who begat who begat whom. No trail will lead up to my genetic dooryard. There will be a closed door with a cliff dropping off behind it.

Sometimes it feels so foolhardy. Instead of raising children I raise the past onto the mantel of the present. For me, to trust stories means to worry notebooks and tapes and random details from childhood into words. It is what I do instead of breed. I am a son who has no son writing about a father and his father and his father and his father. This dark line trails off the page, but it comes as close as I will ever get to continuing the family tradition.

The
Inheritance
of
Autumn

In November my father will be dead forty years. Each year as the planet cools and the leaves drop across upstate South Carolina, I remember him. In remembering my father, I dig with a spade, try to unearth his absence. Lately this absence has taken on the force of a haunting. I have written poems and stories where my dead father appears to give me advice, correct old habits, finish unfinished business. In my dead father's absence he has become a presence. He has come to inhabit this place—Spartanburg, South Carolina—as clearly as we inhabited the town of his death.

For me November is like what the old Dutch called *Slaght-maand,* or "slaughter month," the time livestock were slain and salted for winter. The Saxons called it *Wind-maand,* or "wind-month," because in November the fishermen drew their boats to shore and gave up fishing until the next year. "No fruit, no flowers, no leaves, no birds!—November!" wrote the English poet Thomas Hood.

Attending to the place of November in my own turning year, I often try to imagine my dead father doing something simple, such as peeling the last homegrown cucumber of the season with his pocketknife, watering sunflowers, placing the wedding ring on my mother's finger, or changing the oil in his Willis Jeep at the Southern Pines, North Carolina, service station he ran for years. I too plant sunflowers, and it is too easy to note how they grow huge and yellow all summer and collapse under migrating songbirds in November, when the seed heads dry and the seeds fall to the ground.

I can hear the temporary melancholy in the sentences I've just written. It is the sound of November approaching through the ether. It is the sound of words turning heavy with the coming cold. There is also my natural inclination to head off sadness, make a joke, assure the reader that I am not melancholy and that this is not a melancholy essay. But what else could be written about November? For me it is always a darkening month, even in South Carolina. When November leaves, winter is only twenty-one days ahead. Outside, the streetlights come on early. As I wander downward toward sleep, I notice the sheets are already cool. This is how a year in a place takes on a soul, deepens into meaning.

There are the details of our different lives: My father was born on a farm in coastal North Carolina before the First World War in deep winter; I was born on the cusp of November in the North Carolina sand hills two hundred miles northeast of here. If my father had not taken his life, my mother would never have moved us back to Spartanburg, South Carolina, this mill town where she grew up. It is my mother's place—my grandparents were married in a church three blocks to my west—but it has become, through time and habit, my place. Without my father's death, I would literally be someplace else today.

My father's death placed me psychologically: I am the son of a suicide. I live in a place of abandonment, where the address is always uncertain. The weather is never predictable or steady for the son of a suicide. Out there somewhere on the horizon is the Great Depression. Some sons of suicides (and I am one) are the world's Tom Joads, and every day could end up a dust bowl.

"Father/land," I've written often at the top of a journal page and never been quite sure how to play out the lost drama of place and family and abandonment. Somehow land is part of the pattern for both my father and me. I've always seen him as a man who lost his place, and I'm one who has worked to recover mine through writing. Just this morning I went through twenty years of journal entries for November, trying to get some fix on whether I've always been depressed in the fall. It looks as if the answer is no. There were stretches of November where I was in love or traveling or writing with great concentration. Other years I have mentioned his absence, though, and reflected on our shared space: "Father seems to be my sea," I wrote in 1997. "I'm soaked in it." And just last year: "My father's patterns. What are they?" Judging from the journals, reflection seems something I have grown into lately and this November will be its culmination in some logical way. I was only five when he died. I'm forty-four now, and this month I finally did the math on the back of an envelope: my father was born on January 14, 1915, and he died on November 15, 1959, aged forty-four years, ten months and one day. On August 29 I will be the age my father was when he died. By November I will be well past him.

Will that settle his death for me? Will it ever be settled? How does one understand a death, any death, much less a father's suicide with no note left behind? I know all the details: My father came back disturbed from World War II and spent time in an army hospital; he attempted suicide several times in the twelve years after the war until his death; he struggled with depression and alcohol; he finally succeeded in ending his life idling in the driveway of our home in Southern Pines on the morning of November 15, 1959, a vacuum cleaner hose tucked in the window of the car; my mother found him.

—

Soon after my father's death my mother moved us back to South Carolina to be near her people. My father's sisters kept in touch with letters and Christmas cards. I knew that when I was old enough, I would travel on my own to visit my father's family. In 1964, when I turned ten, I rode the Greyhound bus from Spartanburg to Wilson by myself. After my aunts knew I could do it, I went every summer. They paid for the ticket. From Spartanburg to Raleigh and then the local line to Wilson. It took all day. Much of the day I rode through tobacco fields.

My Aunt Eula would pick me up at the station in Wilson. She drove a practical, white Oldsmobile, called the trunk "the boot." When I opened the door to put my bag in, the cool air in the car smelled of tobacco smoke. Usually my Aunt Alice, the old maid, was with Aunt Eula. My mother knew that Aunt Alice had spent part of her life in the state hospital because of a man. I knew that the man came to visit Aunt Alice sometimes and always brought intricately carved wood projects he had made himself, a shelf for trinkets; a box for jewelry. They sat in the living room of Aunt Eula's house on Greene Street and talked. I've worried about my father's melancholy, my Aunt Alice's stints in the state hospital. Inheritances come in many forms.

It is mostly through his eight brothers and sisters that I have filled in my father's life from childhood through marriage. He grew up on an eastern North Carolina tobacco farm that had been in his family for two hundred years, drove a school bus for the county upon graduation from Lane School, a rural school named for his family. Then he tried to farm a crop of tobacco but enlisted in the army as soon as there was a war to take him away.

"Your father never talked about it," my mother always says when I ask her about his war years. The only personal story I have ever heard (from aunts and uncles) was that he was lost from his unit in Africa, and when he returned, they told him that his mother had died back home.

My father was close to his mother, and it comes out in one of two war letters I have tucked away. The letters were given to me by an aunt, my father's sister-in-law. One was written from England the February before the invasion. He wrote it sitting next to a generator used to supply lights. "I can hardly think for the noise," he said. The handwriting shows a man with good grammar and spelling ("furlough" is spelled correctly, and he never says "to" when he means "too") but one who did not use periods to end sentences. In the second letter he is writing to console a friend on the death of her husband. He tells her she has to "hold up" as he has since the death of his mother. He proves sensitive and articulate beyond what I would have expected of a farm boy from eastern North Carolina.

Sensitivity had its price, it seems. First there was the hospital after the war and then there was his drinking.

My father had grown up a farmer's boy tied to place, and when he left the army, I have been told, he tried to come home, to put in a crop of tobacco on his own. He was one of the younger of six sons and so maybe the farm was something to escape from. I know he left and ended up in Southern Pines, a town a hundred miles inland on U.S. Highway 1, the north-south route from New York to Florida in the days before interstates.

Maybe, one friend has suggested, it was simply that my father was good with cars. Maybe that's why he opened a gas station. "Maybe he wasn't good with farms," my friend laughed as I told him my theories of my father's flight to Southern Pines.

Southern Pines is where he met my mother, who had come north with her young daughter (my half-sister) after marrying and divorcing a soldier in Spartanburg. Her father was from a farm near Southern Pines. It was what Bob Dylan would call "a simple twist of fate" that placed my mother and father—two tortured souls from different worlds—so close together after the war. I know that he had ten good years before the bypass closed him down. Maybe it's just that he didn't see the future approaching—interstates, his own demons, and the death of the slow life.

It was getting cool in central North Carolina when my father died. He had put his garden to bed for the season by the time he wandered out in the yard and took his life in the early morning of November 15, 1959. Maybe a mess or two of collards survived in his garden plot, but most of his vegetables had played out over September and October. In Southern Pines, there had not been a frost by mid-November. "Killing frost," the farmers call the first frost.

Three decades after my father died, I was in Southern Pines visiting my cousins. Judy, the youngest daughter of my father's brother Julian, went into a back room, brought out a yellowed newspaper. She explained how she collects old patterns and had been at a yard sale checking for dress patterns in a box. The bottom of the box was lined with old newspapers, and at the bottom of one box she had discovered this one. "It was staring up at me. I couldn't miss it." She unfolded the paper and pointed out a small news story of her uncle's suicide. "Violence centers on Moore," the headline read. She shook her head, said, "You should have it."

This year, the paper is forty years old. The yellowed column of the newspaper relates a brief narrative of my father's death. The anonymous writer explains how my father was found dead the day before, Saturday, November 15th around 5:15 A.M. in the driveway of his home. "The windows were closed and a vacuum cleaner tube connected with the exhaust pipe had been placed in the car." There, in the next paragraph is the name of my mother, who had found him. "She told the coroner that her husband had gone to bed at the usual time and she did not know when he'd gotten up." My sister's name, Sandy, and my childhood name, Johnny, appear among the survivors.

That Saturday was a day of death: the paper reports a plane had plunged into the Gulf of Mexico killing all forty-two on board. The whole state of Kansas was mobilized in a manhunt for the "shotgun killers" of a wealthy farmer, his wife, and two teenage children, the murders that would become the basis of *In Cold Blood*. In the brief story reporting my father's suicide, the paper also disclosed the deaths of a baby from accidental poisoning and of another child struck and killed on a highway. There was also local news: hog prices in Raleigh, the 117th birthday of the last surviving veteran of the Civil War, girls vying for the title of "Miss Yuletide."

My father's last watch is curled and quiet in a top drawer where my mother keeps her insurance papers. It hasn't run in years, a cheap square-faced Timex with a brittle leather band. Sometimes, I take it out and wonder when it stopped ticking and why it wasn't buried with him. I asked my mother once and she explained how my father hated to wear a watch, a trait I've inherited.

———

I can't imagine how it must have felt, the nothingness of morning when my mother wandered out of sleep to find my father gone from bed and sensed the terrible idling engine in the dark driveway. The last, huge sunflower heads nodding in the November cold. The fogged windows. The knowledge he was gone, finally. He had tried it before—with razor blades. This time there was a deliberateness, a certainty that endures through time to this day. It was my inheritance of autumn, a pattern from birth.

Some sons are given the inheritance of summer, and for those there is a sense of full bloom, lives of fulfilled promise. These men are the bright souls who are never alone. Others are born into the hint of infinite possibility, of bloom, with spring emerging in every moment. Others, it seems, walk into life already in deep cold.

I think my father was winter's child, and he could not see his way through another one. Maybe that's explanation enough. He made me autumn's child. With his suicide he gave me the month of November with its warm days and cool nights. This year I mark his final passing with a last harvest, the fruit from my father's vine.

My mother says my father always weeded his garden. By November it was plowed under and ready for winter. If I dropped dead tomorrow, I would leave no will behind, only sunflowers, and a poorly weeded garden already turning yellow in the autumn heat. Unlike my father I am lazy in the rituals of civic life. I pay my bills late. I might vote as soon as not. My possessions—some property, thousands of books, clothes, furniture, a truck—would be divided up somehow. I would hope my sister would deal with it all. My mother has seen enough tragedy for one lifetime. My father's legacy to me is that it is never beyond me, the idea that life could end as it began, in sudden certainty, surprising as a spark. I wish I had inherited something more useful from my father: say, his love for farming. It seems a connection to earth and its weather is harder to pass along than seasonal melancholy.

Some summers, when I visited my father's family, I worked in their fields, cropping tobacco or bucking hay. It was not work I enjoyed, though now, looking back, it is work I'm glad I had the privilege to do. The idea of farm, Wendell Berry reminds us, originally included the idea of household.

The world has changed so much since my father died that I had fun writing poems in which I challenged him with situations I thought he would not recognize. In the poems I took my dead father's ghost to a movie, to a video poker parlor, to the beach. Each time he surprised me. He was a man who chose to leave the world of a family farm—a world that had not changed much in two hundred years—first for a war and then for some sort of dream I'll never know. He knew a great deal about adaptability. I am a man who chooses to leave manual labor behind for the fluency of words and books. I wonder often if my father would understand my working these essays the way he worked his father's fields with a hoe or a valve job with a socket wrench.

Slurry

The nurse says my mother is a hard study, that the plaque in her arteries is very dense. It causes "acoustic shadowing," a condition that makes it difficult to estimate how much the passage in each carotid artery is blocked. The nurse says, so far there doesn't seem to be much change in the six months since my mother was last in, though it looks as if there is at least a 40 percent blockage in the left artery, a little less in the right. My mother cannot see the picture of her thin neck and the arteries beneath her loose skin. Her head is propped up slightly on a flat, white pillow, and her muscles form a V, the big end accenting her chin. Her blocked carotids run like twin rivers on each side of the rocky ledge of her cervical vertebrae. They carry the oxygenated blood to her brain, branch just below her chin line, and disappear deep into her thinning, gray hair.

"Her vessel disease," my sister calls it. We've been watching my mother's ultrasounds for two years now, her doctor trying to divine my mother's decline in memory, her slowing down so quickly. What governs my mother now is a sense of loss. She has many of the symptoms of someone suffering small strokes—clumsiness, weakness, a searching constantly for words that used to be easy to bend into sentences, jokes, and requests. Today she was confused when we arrived at the hospital: she told one orderly, when we asked directions to the lab, that she was here for a "brain x-ray."

Two years earlier I had sat and waited as my mother went through cataract surgery in this same hospital. It was meant to be a renewal. The doctor, a man who traveled over from a nearby town, performed a dozen of the expensive surgeries each day. "Routine," is how my sister, a nurse, had described the surgery. As he performed the laser surgery, he had been short with her. She'd had trouble keeping her head still and once he had yelled, "No movement!" At least that's how she reported the incident on the ride home.

The eye surgery had been a success—at least that's what we

thought—and my mother was able to read small print without glasses for the first time in years. In spite of the success, something depressed her about the surgery, and it took days of talking with her for me to get to the bottom of it. Finally, sitting with her in her front room, she said, "Johnny, when that doctor took out my old lenses, he put back in little pieces of glass. Your eyes are the windows of your soul. Well, I feel like they've taken my soul away. When people look in now, they can't see me. Something's gone." She began to cry.

"Mama, if your soul has windows, then there must be a door," I said, struggling to make sense out of her story. "Where is the door to your soul?"

"My throat, I guess," she said.

"Well, you need to keep talking; that's the way people can get into your soul now."

I spent two nights in this hospital thirteen years ago. It was October and I was thirty-three, a river guide and a freelance writer with plans to catch a flight to Costa Rica in a week to live cheaply, paddle, and write a winter's worth of articles about that country's then-emerging ecotravel industry. It sounds romantic, but looking back, I was as close to the edge as one could be, living on adrenaline, youth, and five thousand bucks a year. I had no permanent address, no suit of clothes that demanded ironing, no wife or children. It was as if I believed life would ripen into fullness if only I followed my passions. The old Arab proverb says, "Trust in God, but tie your camel." Well, at thirty-three my camels were roaming free in the desert, and I didn't even know it.

Then I came into town for one last weekend before leaving the country, decided to play basketball with the guys at the college. Two or three trips down the court and I was sprawled under the basket with a ruptured Achilles tendon. I felt it pop, and it was just like you hear it is: my foot flopping free, my tendon withdrawn up my calf. One of my friends swears the first thing I said as I hit the floor was, "How am I going to pay for this?"

They let me in the hospital in spite of not having health insurance. I had the surgery and a good doctor sewed the tendon back together, plastered my leg from hip to toe. When I left my room on crutches two days later, my bill was seven thousand dollars. "Like buying a used car," I thought as I saw the bill. I told them I would pay it off on time. I told them I was good for it, though I was unemployed and obviously not headed to Costa Rica to kayak.

Where would I go? I was virtually homeless, most of my belongings stored in the back of my pickup truck in anticipation of the trip to Costa Rica. I couldn't return to the rafting company where I had worked the summer. The housing there was not winterized, and I would have the huge cast on my leg for four weeks. My sister drove me to my mother's house, and my mother took me in, as mothers will do. She set me up in the spare bedroom, the very space I had occupied as a teen.

My mother remembers that time as one of festival and activity. Friends from the college came to visit daily, to sit with me in the den and talk. I remember it as a time of great depression. I was embarrassed that my friends at both NOC and the college had taken up a collection to help pay my medical bills. I was a man with only one safety net—his mother. It was difficult to return home, a failed son who had discovered his own personal Achilles' heel purely by accident.

We shared that house until February when I was headed up to Interlochen, Michigan, where I had set up a little teaching job for the spring. By that time my leg would be out of the cast and I would be on the road to recovery, at least physically.

I watch my mother on the table, think about how much she has changed in thirteen years. And me? I'm teaching now, with health insurance. The hospital bill was paid off in three years with some help. "Not the kindness of strangers," I always joke, "but even better, the kindness of friends." I often remind my mother of the time we spent together, two stubborn adults sharing a house, and she always laughs, says it was good for us both, to learn patience and tolerance, she at an advanced age, and me advancing into middle age.

"You are a good son," she says when I complain about my selfish pursuit of my own uncertain goals.

I go back and sit down, listen from across the room as my mother's blood slurs and pulses under the head of the ultrasound and ends up as an image on the computer screen. It is so much like run-off after a big rain, this blood stream. The sound, I think to myself, is like water coming in bursts through a drain pipe. The nurse speaks steadily into the machine, noting a series of measurements—velocities and directions—for the doctor to review later. I walk over and look at the picture again, lean close, try to read the message in the broken, black lines of my mother's blood stream pulsing through the constricted passages that are her seventy-three-year-old arteries.

She has smoked a pack of cigarettes a day since she was a girl in the 1930s. Over sixty years of Viceroy smoke coursing through her lungs, yet she is persistent in keeping up the habit. It has become obvious that she will die smoking. I keep seeing the image of the man with throat cancer who smokes through the ragged hole in his throat. My mother has that sort of stubbornness. When I picked her up this morning, she was waiting by the door, cigarette in hand, fighting for that last drag before the long ride downtown, the waiting room's flavorless air, the hour-long procedure.

"You're an old seventy-three," I lean over and tell her. She smiles, wrapped in the heather-colored sweater I brought her from Ireland. She looks naked without her glasses, her gray hair exposed and bent slightly out of place by the pillow, the hair, she has told a woman in the waiting room, she keeps covered with a hat because she can't get to the hairdresser often enough. In this age when men and women in their seventies are often running marathons and swimming lakes, my mother walks shakily with a cane and is shrunken to a frail eighty-eight pounds.

My mother makes no excuses. She knows that at seventy-three she is a system poorly maintained, a fence never mended, a farm gone weedy from neglect. The left palm of genetics has grasped the right palm of habit. Teeth gone, bones brittle, muscles atrophied to flaccid flesh, but she still blooms like a rose when someone does something kind for her. Behind her laughter, her full human capacity to love and be loved, however, is a flower quickly wilting. Had she known, would she have paid attention? Would she have stopped smoking, fought off the demons of alcohol, borrowed money to go to the dentist?

The room is dark and my mother lies on the table. I can see the nurse sitting behind her in a green smock. She is very patient, even as my mother moves her hands up and down, disturbing the image of the blood through the arteries displayed on her screen. "Still, still please," the nurse croons when the image is compromised by the motion. My mother obeys, lies as still as possible on the bright silver exam table covered with the black blanket. She has always been obedient to those in medicine, "the healing arts." They are competent and kindly. The nurse moves the head of the instrument—like a sea snake loose in her hand—around on my mother's neck and says, "Just two more measurements, Mrs. Lane, and we'll be done." My mother glances up. She likes to be called "Mrs. Lane." I can see in her face she is relieved it's almost over.

I get up again, join my mother at the table, look down at her fingers bent at odd angles by years of arthritis, think about how much I have inherited from my mother, her once-dark hair, her sense of humor, her love of good stories. There is also her high blood pressure, which shows up in me from time to time when I'm under stress; her tendency to put off, to defer when money is involved; and her stubbornness, how she can hold on to something long after it's time to let go. Right now she's probably thinking of a smoke, a deep draw filling her lungs, comforting her in this time of great trouble. I never took to smoking, but as I sit in the vascular lab, I wonder at the rich plaques building up in my own self as I age. What dark flotsam? What sluices through my life, my blood, swirls on the edges of the current?

Last night I went to dinner with an affluent friend, a conservative businessman with a fondness for feeding liberals, and argued with him good-naturedly about the government, especially taxes. "Who knows better how to spend my money than me?" he said as he rolled a good red wine in a crystal glass. "It's all about efficiency."

My host laughed when I told him I thought efficiency was over-rated. Then, as a form of explanation, I told him a story, how as a paperboy for three years in high school I had learned nothing of the primary economic values that are often cited as character building. My mother had risen at 5 A.M. and rolled my papers for me, and then I had thrown them on the three or four streets closest to ours. One hundred twenty papers, weekly and Sunday, rain or shine for three years. It should have been good training. It should have made me a thrifty boy. "All it trained me to do was rise at dawn," I said and laughed.

Yes, I did it for the money, but I didn't do it very well. I paid the paper bill each month and added the subscribers that mailed in their money to my total take. "Of the ones that were left, I only collected enough of the route to pay for my dates and gas," I explained to my friend, the president of a large company, the holder of mutual funds and savings accounts. "Anytime I needed ten dollars, I would head out and knock on a few doors. I was a sloppy bookkeeper. I probably left one hundred dollars out on the route each month for three years."

Yes, sloppy is how I would describe it. This sloppiness made me feel in charge. It made me feel powerful. I wasn't a slave to numbers, money pouches, and columns. I kept change and folding money in my pocket and spent it as needed. I cashed the checks as they came in. (To this day I still don't balance my checkbook and my wallet is always empty, money wadded in a front pocket.) There could have been people on the route who never paid me. It must have felt like some sort of undeserved monthly gift wrought by neglect, a paper arriving out of nowhere and a paperboy never asking to be paid.

My friend smiled and shook his head, went back to wine and politics. He had no answer for this anecdotal lesson in failed economy, a small business that should have perished from its lack of efficiency. Politics was an easier target: the faraway politicians and the laws governing our lives clear criminals because of the way they clog up a simple system. He would say my paperboy system was working because I could choose what to do with my money, to leave it on the street or not. "Individuals do well and have clear title to the fruits of their labors," he explained again. "I know how best to spend my money."

That wasn't my point. What I was really explaining with my story of bungled thrift was a resentment against money that had already built up in my blood at fourteen, turning me away from the simple lessons of the free market. It was as if I had decided I would remain forever in the ranks of the poor, seeing my mother's inheritance somehow as that. She had stayed poor, and so would I. I am forty-five now and purely middle class, a college professor who owns his own home, but I still maintain no savings account, no mutual funds, no sense of a future made comfortable by thrift and efficiency.

My mother's old age came on at seventy like a storm. It was as if an aging bomb had gone off in her blood. She lost weight. She grew dizzy when she walked. She diminished in activity. Her house grew heavy under cigarette smoke and dust as she sat longer in her lounger in the front room. In her early sixties, she had been robust, though not independent. She drove out on the west side, walked at the mall, even met a man there who took her on motorcycle rides in the mountains. She was active and her focus was more outward than now.

Later that decade a wreck stopped her driving. The brown Oldsmobile sat in the driveway for two years with a bent fender before it was obvious she would not drive again, and we sold it to an interested passerby. With the car gone, my mother became more dependent on us all to pick up groceries. Though she still cooked large family dinners every Sunday, she sometimes complained about the hot work in front of the stove.

At that point there was nothing physical to pin it on. My mother went to the doctor often and the report was that she was holding up well for a woman who had struggled with deep and persistent poverty, had smoked all her life, had fought alcohol in her middle years, and had become sedentary in her later ones. She had told me once she thought she would die at fifty-four, the age her mother had died of a stroke. As soon as she cruised through that milestone, her drinking had stopped. She had a new, long-term lease, and suddenly old age seemed a possibility.

As my mother's activity diminished, my sister and I grew resentful over having to manage our own lives plus hers. She was short with us on the phone. We complained about the cigarette smoke and used it as an excuse as to why we could not come visit. As seventy approached, my mother became more and more isolated. Her only regular outlet was a weekly, Friday-night trip to Wal-Mart and Krispy Kreme with her sister and brother-in-law. Her only contact with family increasingly became the Sunday dinner that she hosted in her smoky house.

This morning, while sitting in the waiting room of the vascular lab, I asked my mother which of the family's Sunday recipes she missed cooking the most. "The chicken and dumplings," she said. "I put a can of cream of celery soup in the gravy. No one else does that." I know that my mother's chicken and dumplings takes an entire morning to prepare, and she has not attempted the dish in three years. I used to sit and watch her roll the biscuit dough on the counter and cut the thin dough into strips. We would sit and talk in the kitchen some Sunday mornings. "I used to boil whole chickens," she says. "That was before they sold the chicken strips in the store. In those days my chicken and dumplings had white and dark meat."

Now that I'm a college teacher, I have some money. I often think that I should be supporting my mother, who supported me so many years on a pauper's income. I try to do what I can in small ways. Beside my bed is a red basket into which I empty my change each night. I drain my two pockets of all the quarters, dimes, nickels, and pennies. They pile up daily like sand down a stream. Each Christmas, after fifty-two weeks, I wrap the basket up and give it to my mother. She has come to expect it.

In January she sits in the den and rolls the coins, snugging the silver and copper in tight new wrappers with her bent, yet precise, fingers. When finished, she piles the rolled pennies, dimes, quarters, and nickels in their separate stacks on the dusty, dining room table and counts them. Some years there's as much as three hundred dollars in the basket. Other years, when I've raided the basket, strip-mining the layers for quarters to feed the soda machines, there is as little as a hundred fifty.

My mother won't listen when I suggest we take the coins to one of those rolling machines and simply pour it all in. "That would take the fun out of it," she says. "I like to know how much I got."

I think of the Christmas basket as I stand beside her bed, the procedure winding down. "You're done, Mrs. Lane," the nurse says and my mother starts the leisurely drift toward departure. We sit her up, help her on with her shoes, hand her her cane. With her glasses back on she finally looks like herself again, and we head down the corridor and ride the elevator to the lobby.

Riding home from the hospital, my mother seems happy there is no change in her condition, but she asks few questions about the specific outcomes of the tests. I am more anxious than she is to find out what is moving through her old, slurried blood. I ask her what she will do the rest of the day. She says she'll sit in her big chair, watch TV, begin reading the stack of novels brought in weekly by a worker from the library. My mother has grown close to the young woman who has started bringing the books, and she coaches the woman toward her peculiar tastes. I ask my mother what this week's pile has to offer. "Stories about the kings and queens of England." She smiles. I think about the books as I unfasten the seat belt, help my mother out of the truck's high cab. I imagine my mother sitting in her chair, disappearing into each book, a neglected field. "Am I shut-in or homebound?" she asks as I walk her to the door. "They have to know for the form."

The

Ice

Storm

The ice storm moved through the upstate on Saturday evening, shellacking trees and power lines. As the storm approached, my mood changed. A little excitement crept in. Of course, being a poet, I had to think of Robert Frost's poem "Birches," where the speaker explains that swinging does not bend trees down to stay, "Ice-storms do that."

Weather is never only what it seems. It always has that ability to make us reflect, take stock of what's in our emotional pantry. It's not the days that have the nine on the comfort index we remember. It's the ones that don't even chart, hovering down around zero.

This past weekend "The Wedge" (cold Arctic air) was trapped against the rounded shoulders of the Blue Ridge, and moist air from the Gulf pushed over the cold. It was a rare, but classic, Piedmont situation (we get our winter weather secondhand from Atlanta), and even the Weather Channel's anchor, a suited woman gesturing at a nonexistent map, seemed excited. It was going to be a "significant weather event," and, damn, it was all happening too fast for the network to develop color graphics, theme music, and logo.

We do not live in a place where winter is a constant visitor, so any unusual weather quickly becomes epic, metaphoric, symbolic. We give it capital letters, Ice Storm '99, The Year of The Big Freeze, The Swift Strike of the Icy Hammer of the Gods. Our memorable season is summer, where heat thickens at summer solstice and a blanket of humidity settles in June and stays until the equinox in September. This year it seemed that winter itself was on vacation somewhere far north. Thanksgiving, I was still in shorts. Mid-December, there were impatiens still blooming near the front walk.

The afternoon the ice storm hit, I was at Betsy's watching a football game on TV. We knew there was weather approaching, so we scanned the available media for information. Betsy loves storms, and she wasn't going to let this one come in without watching it all the way. We went outside and looked at the sky. It was gray and close overhead. By early afternoon the little plunking sound of sleet had begun. We knew before it hit we were in for some weather.

When the rain began to fall in sheets, Frost's poem came back again: "Often you must have seen them / Loaded with ice a sunny winter morning / After a rain." I thought of how I had not seen them often and of how rare an event an ice storm is in the upstate. "They click upon themselves / As the breeze rises," I recited as we felt the leaves of shrubs already heavy with ice just outside the front door.

Good-bye to the certainty of cable TV reception. That was our first convenience to go. Icing on top of Mount Pisgah, and the certainty of that football game we'd waited all day to see went black just as Doug Flutie heaved a long one downfield. It was time to consider going home and waiting it out. We talked about driving in such weather. We agreed it was not the norm. "I'm the kind of southerner who slides into things when the roads get slick," Betsy said. "You know, the ones that Yankees dread." We hugged, Betsy and I, and said goodbye for the evening as the ice storm settled on us.

I locked the wheels of my 4x4 truck and scraped the ice off the windshield with a cassette case. This is South Carolina. Few but those obsessed with any emergency carry the long winter scraping wand in their vehicle. I engaged the gears and cranked the heat onto high defrost. Outside it was a winter wonderland. Cars crept along the street and wheels made that swirring sound. For a moment, I had a nightmare vision of not getting home (a few miles across town): What if every Suburban-driving mom in Spartanburg decided at this very moment to take her huge, safe machine to the store for one final shot at milk and bread?

Driving home, everybody was slowed to a crawl. There was a woman behind Converse College whose Ford Fiesta had skated down a slight incline into a power pole. Someone had stopped to help. They stood huddled by the fender, admiring the crease. There were icy skid marks from her lane to the pole. She had a shawl pulled over her head and looked more like a character from a Thomas Hardy novel caught forever on a moor than someone from subtropical Spartanburg.

On Pine Street members of the Weather Wild Bunch kept up their speed as cars sluiced past spewing gales of ice and water. How could they run so fast in this weather? The freezing rain pounded on the enameled hood of my truck and thickened on my windshield wipers in spite of the motion. I could barely see the big, digital thermometer at the old Kmart plaza that said twenty-eight degrees. We had dropped for good into the Land of Freezing. The Wedge was hard against us.

That night my power stayed on, but sixty thousand in the area weren't so lucky. The houses winked out all around me. Trees snapped and exploded as the ice thickened on the limbs. Wires went crazy in the street. Transformers shorted out and an eery, green light filled the sky. The sound of the ice storm was like a battlefield as the overburdened limbs snapped off. "Like hand grenades," a friend explained. "Like an endless round of target practice with some large ordinance."

I missed Betsy and worried about her, wished I had braved the ice storm to go back and pick her up. All night, in my dreams, I went out the back door, traversed the icy deck and steps, and checked the thickness of the ice on a chain-link fence. It seemed important somehow to know how much ice had gathered there.

The next morning my power was on but the radio was dead, the signal lost to ice. By 8 A.M. the temperature was up to thirty-two and the roads were already slushy, though an inch of sleet and ice still covered all the yards. Down my street every tree had lost at least a limb, and some more. One huge oak two yards down had split near the top and fallen over the sidewalk to form an icy bridge. Betsy called to say her power was off. She'd slept the night in front of her fireplace with her beagle and gas logs to warm her. Were the roads clear? Had I heard any news of the storm's severity? We talked like refugees from a war. Could I come get her? "There's got to be coffee in my future," she said.

I locked the hubs on the truck and picked her up. We rubber-necked around the war zone, checking on damage in her particular zip code. We laughed about rich people calling poor people to clean up their yards and all the money that would change hands. "Who knows what the northern end of the county looks like?" Betsy said.

In one old Spartanburg neighborhood (one that had seen an ice storm or two) the streets were heavy with limbs and we drove an obstacle course to get past power lines. In one yard a huge water oak had toppled and a crowd of mourners stood with cameras. The tree looked like a fallen dinosaur from Jurassic Park. Going over, it had pulled a flat scab of driveway with it. The hole looked like a bomb crater. In another yard a power pole had snapped halfway and the T-top dangled by lines over the street. "All this from ice," I said as we drove around.

It was still Sunday in spite of the storm, so we went to Betsy's church. The men arrived in big boots, the women in pants. It was warm in the old church, and the music lifted us as ice crashed on the slate roof and piled next to the stones outside. After the service we drove around in my truck, a moving feast of disaster, checking on all our friends. Most were without power. Most were making the best of it with gas grills, hot chocolate, and comforters. Pine tops were sprawled next to cars, just missing an insurance settlement by a foot, and backyards were thick with fallen branches. A policeman told us that a thousand trees had come down over roads all over the county. They would have to be cleared before the lines could be reattached for power.

I dropped Betsy off at a friend's house. There were limbs in her yard but she still had power. Betsy planned to camp there in the guest bedroom until the power returned. Betsy's boys would be home from a winter beach trip by midafternoon, and she would tell them the long story of the ice storm they had missed, how their house had gone dark and cold, and their mother had curled on the foldout bed in front of the gas logs with Toby the beagle hound.

As I drove home in the cold and slush, I saw the most surreal scene, something out of a movie: twenty-nine yellow power trucks passing at one intersection, headed out into the crippled county to work on people's electricity. I realized how much we depend on our grid of comfort. I admitted, safe in my truck, that community is thick and a good dose of weather can test it to the core.

The ice storm had written its signature clearly across the upstate. "It was the fourth worst storm in the last quarter century," the newly reestablished Weather Channel told us. I tell these stories because Bill McKibben says in *The End of Nature* that talk about the weather is our "oldest way of saying that deep down all is right with the world." McKibben explains how each season offers not only its surprises but also its predictable weather, forming what Edwin Way Teale has called "the rounded year." After the weekend ice storm my year feels rounded, curving now toward spring in the circling seasons. Somehow, I know that the ice storm is what we will talk about over lunch today and tomorrow. It's the adversity that keeps us together.

Confluence:

Pacolet

River

The Blue Ridge Mountains, visible from Spartanburg, South Carolina, on a clear day, have always had the nostalgic force of a song for my family. Stories told by my aunts and uncles in the early 1960s confirmed that we had come from there. They told me how my great-grandparents migrated down from mountainous Rutherford County to work Spartanburg's numerous Piedmont cotton mills at the end of the nineteenth century. With time off from shift work and a little gas in the ramshackle car, my mother would often take me back up there to cool down on a summer day.

On those childhood outings, we traveled up U.S. Highway 176, the original road from Spartanburg into the mountains. As it approaches the mountain front, the highway follows the course of the North Pacolet River. As a child, I loved how the narrow two-lane climbed the slopes of the Big Warrior, Little Warrior, and Cedar mountains in steep switchbacks. Local historians say the road follows an ancient game trail along the dizzy gradient of the river and marks the descent of an Indian trading path walked for thousands of years to reach the Piedmont and the coast two hundred miles away. On the other side of the river is one of the steepest railroad grades in the eastern United States, and now, just east of the old highway, Interstate 26 carries commerce quickly across the flank of Tryon Mountain and over Howard Gap onto the Hendersonville plateau.

My mother would load me into our beat-up, cantaloupe-colored DeSoto convertible with the white ragtop and head out for those cooler mountains. It was water she was headed toward, cool water falling over stones. We would pick up one or two of her brothers in Saxon, a mill village on the city's outskirts. As my mother says, back then, they were "into loafing," young boys often laying off from relentless work in the cotton mills.

Often one of the twins, with his white tee, ducktailed hair (it was the 1960s), and a Pall Mall in his mouth, would drive the DeSoto. The other twin would sit in the passenger seat twisting the AM from station to station. Mama and I would sit in the back, her black hair pulled back secure from the hot Piedmont wind by a patterned, rayon scarf. After crossing into North Carolina and negotiating most of the Saluda Grade, a switchback highway, my uncle would park by the side of the road in a narrow pull-off crowded on one side by a sweating gneiss cliff and on the other by the highway. For each trip Mama packed fried chicken, deviled eggs, potato salad, and sweet tea for me. Maybe there would be some hidden Budweiser in the trunk. We would sit roadside at a small concrete table and picnic.

Then we'd work our way down to the roaring North Pacolet and I would slide over the rocks left by ice wedging and flood in the channel. Back then, I never thought of that river as going somewhere, falling toward sea level. It was always as if it had been laid out like a carnival ride (or today's water parks) simply for my enjoyment—big, slick rocks; falling water; overhanging rhododendron. When the sun dropped below the gorge walls, we would retrace our steps up to the highway, pack up the DeSoto, and head back down into the mill village.

These are my earliest memories of water—of escape and relief. It's said the Cherokee, who claimed what would become Spartanburg County as their territory, went regularly to water to purify. For them each river was "the Long Man" with its head in the mountains and its feet dangling in the ocean far away. I look back now at the irony of that cantaloupe-colored DeSoto, named after the first Spanish explorer who in 1539 looped decisively through this territory. Traveling a Piedmont river like the Pacolet (probably the Catawba), DeSoto set the tone for the future, looking for gold and trailing a herd of pigs.

It's now November, and I am back on the Pacolet, though thirty miles downstream from my childhood picnic spot. I'm floating the river this time, not playing among boulders and waterfalls. At this point along its course the Pacolet has become wide and shallow with very little exposed rock as it makes its way over the wide Carolina Piedmont, an area of steep hills but few extremes in elevation or scenery. I've realized recently that I've somehow missed this river my entire life. As an expert kayaker, I found challenging rivers were always somewhere else, never close by. Twenty years ago, when I began white-water kayaking, I always had to head west from Spartanburg and climb into the mountains where there were steeper gradients. (Once it leaves the mountain front, the Pacolet drops only an average of five feet a mile. In contrast, the Chattooga, seventy miles west, can drop as much as two hundred feet per mile.) In this way my kayaking adventures reflected my youthful picnics. Now, I'm older, less driven by adrenaline, and paying attention to nearby places as never before. Piedmont rivers like the Pacolet are appealing for the first time, and I've made a vow to paddle all of them over the next few seasons.

There's not much time left this year to keep my vow. We've already had the first hard frost. The tulip poplar leaves have already turned yellow and fallen. I am paddling with Betsy and her ten-year-old son, Russell. We've packed a lunch of sandwiches, apples, and soft drinks. It's my equivalent of the childhood picnics, minus the beer. We are on the northern edge of Spartanburg, in a rural area near Interstate 85. We plan to put in with our sea kayaks and float the river from Bud Arthur Bridge Road to the old abandoned Converse cotton mill where my uncle Tommy once worked, a distance of about five river miles. Though I've never paddled it before, I've been told the stretch, just downstream from where the river crosses the Interstate (maybe thirty miles from the river's origin) is marked by only one road crossing, a house or two, and a mining operation for sand. I know the current will be steady, and there is abundant wildlife: wood ducks, mallards, great blue herons, hawks, and kingfishers frequent the stretch.

The stretch will make for a pleasant fall paddle. The air temperature is in the seventies. The river is maybe a hundred feet wide, clear, and two feet deep. Looking at my topo map before we left, I could see that the river sweeps through two large meanders. The bunched-up lines tell me there are steep, north-facing bluffs along the way, probably covered with mountain laurel (a species common to the Blue Ridge, but no stranger to cool Piedmont river bluffs) and dark hardwood. Though we will only be three miles from the city limits of Spartanburg, I know it will feel like we are surrounded by wooded country thick with mature oaks and poplars.

A friend will pick us up downstream later in the day, so we leave my truck parked near the bridge, slide the brightly colored, plastic kayaks like otters (sometimes still seen on the Pacolet) down the steep, long approach our paddling friends have told us about. I wrestle each kayak down as far as possible and let go. The boats bounce to an angled stop short of the river. I laugh at how difficult it is to get into the flow. "It seems a resource so public should have some sort of access short of skydiving," I say.

When I pause and listen, it's possible to pick up the sound of a small, wild shoal one hundred yards upstream. The water is noisy as it works its angled descent over the exposed country rock; and beyond that, hanging in the air like static, is the sound of hundreds of cars and trucks humming over the expansion joints on the interstate. Just above us is one of the busiest stretches of highway on the East Coast, and yet in a few moments we will push off from shore and Huck-Finn our way downstream in a rhythm as old as any human impulse. Floating, my kayaking friends call it. "Let's go float a river," they say.

On the topo map the Pacolet's two main branches are laid like a tuning fork against the South Carolina Piedmont and the mountains to the west. Along its fifty-mile journey before the confluence with the Broad River in Union County, the river falls over many (though widely spaced) sets of shoals. They are often designated on the map by double bars piercing the blue line of the river. Before railroads rendered the river redundant for transportation, these shoals made long-distance navigation on the Pacolet difficult but created many "mill seats," topography with enough fall to generate power for early industry. This natural power—and the jobs created in the cotton mills—is what drew my family from the mountains to Spartanburg County. It was a confluence of need and geography that formed our connection to this river and its many tributaries.

Along the Saluda Grade, where we had parked to picnic, the north fork of the river falls precipitously for fifteen miles through rhododendron, laurel hells, and large mountain hardwoods (hemlock, sweet birch, white oak) on slopes too steep to log. The North Pacolet's noisy descent now comforts porch sitters in vacation cabins and finally flattens out near Tryon (where F. Scott Fitzgerald spent summers in the mid-1930s) and flows swiftly through old farm country in what's known as "the thermal belt," an area traditionally associated with milder winter temperatures and fewer days of frost, though no one has confirmed this scientifically.

The South Pacolet, the other prong of the tuning fork, is much shorter and less extroverted, falling off the lower slopes of Hogback Mountain as a series of narrow creeks. Then it quickly ceases its mountain song as it meanders quietly among Piedmont hills, abandoned peach orchards, old field succession, and the first hints of suburban sprawl.

Confluence of uses, confluence of memory, I think as we begin our float on the main branch of the river. In high school I waterskied on Lake Bowen, the reservoir formed on the dammed South Pacolet River. Lake Bowen is the source of Spartanburg's drinking water and is tightly ringed with waterfront vacation homes. Powerboats and jet skis rage over the surface three seasons a year, the latter expelling a flume of ruddy lake water as they push into the tiniest coves and inlets.

No one in my family had made it beyond mill work at that time, so we could not afford this affluent form of fun on a regular basis. (Those self-propelled slides down a slick rock during our fried chicken picnics were mostly what I knew of water recreation.) It was through the generosity of high school friends from across town that I once strapped on a ski belt, snapped on water skis, and waited as the Evinrude torqued the prop into high-enough rotation to pull me from the grip of the Pacolet's impounded flow.

I remember gliding over the lake's waters, my arms and legs stiff with exertion. It was an unnatural motion for me. There was too much trust of machinery. It didn't take long for me to tire, swerve, and plow into the lukewarm surface of the water. My buddies cheered as I fell, and they circled the boat back to pick me up. Another boy entered the water for his turn on the skis. Sitting in the stern, recovering my senses, I remember distinctly the sharp bite of petroleum fumes and a rainbow sheen spreading in the bilge pooling in the boat.

Soon after we enter the current in our kayaks, I point upstream toward the sound of the traffic and say that we can paddle up toward the gravel roar of the small rapid and play there. Russell's not appeased. When I say "river," he thinks of rapids. Russell wants his floating to be punctuated by drops and waves. He's young and still on the adrenaline program. He wants to know if there is white water downstream and acts disappointed when I admit it's doubtful. I try to explain that this is not the Blue Ridge but instead a piedmont stream with less of the gradient that produces white water than its mountain counterparts. I guarantee him it will be swift water, though, and he will not have to paddle much. "Just float," I smile. He likes that, and we float into the current and head downstream.

Betsy is glad to hear there won't be any significant white water. The summer before, we were floating a calm mountain river punctuated with occasional rapids, and the curling edge of a wave caught the stern of her boat and dumped her in the cold current. We rescued her, but she still remembers the sting of the cold water. She likes to float but would rather not swim on this warm fall day.

Just downstream from our put-in, as we pass under the Bud Arthur Bridge, we see the first signs of one of the river's historic functions: trash heap for the locals. Someone has thrown two of the newspaper dispensers for the Spartanburg daily paper off the bridge into the river. "Somebody must have frisked them for their quarters," Betsy speculates. I nose my boat up to one. It has been in the river for a long time, unmoved by recent floods. A sheen of algae makes it look more like rock than machine. I peek through the machine's gate into the paper compartment. It's too dark to see anything, but I tell the story of a radial tire a friend picked up on one of the Pacolet's tributaries during a river sweep once. Inside was living a three-pound catfish. With enough time, maybe the river can claim anything.

Remembering the catfish in the tire reminds me that this is a living stream, with bass, bream, riffle beetles, gilled snails, sow bugs, Dobson flies, crayfish—a whole world beneath the surface. It wasn't always so for a river once as impaired as the Pacolet. I know that as recently as the 1960s the textile mills along its length dumped their raw sewage directly into the river. My Uncle Tommy, who worked for decades inspecting cloth and marking it in the cloth room downstream at the Converse cotton mill, likes to tell the story of camping on the wide sandbar at Poole's Bend, a large, sweeping meander on the Pacolet a few miles below the mill. He and some buddies ran a "trout line" and pulled in a washtub full of catfish. "We skinned some to cook over the fire that night. When I opened them up, they smelled like sewage. I couldn't eat catfish for fifty years."

Russell, floating ahead of us, is more interested in the white and turquoise wreck of a jet ski that has somehow landed in the river than in the catfish probably living below its surface. He gets excited. "Maybe we can fix it up?" he asks. I only think about how the infernal machine probably washed downstream from Lake Bowen in flood and how its owner pushed the noisy thing all over the lake in the summer. I am strangely hopeful we'll see more and can pretend they are wreckage of some lost world. "It's like *Planet of the Apes*," Betsy says. "You know, the final scene where they discover the Statue of Liberty and realize they have stumbled into the future."

Floating a river is always a little like wading into another time, especially a river once as heavily settled as the Pacolet. There were once farms along these banks, and now we float through a forest of thirty-year-old poplars, oaks, and sycamores grown toward maturity in the grace period when the farms were abandoned and the mills closed down. The South Carolina Piedmont is a region in the midst of transition: once wilderness, then farmland, but now in an uneasy peace before the war of real estate consumes it all. The contrast between our daily lives—streets, cars, mechanical noise—and the quiet of the postindustrial river is appealing and fragile. As we float for an hour south toward our ride back to town, I think about the scarred yet somehow peaceful landscape this river drains.

I am a native of this place, not merely a visitor or recreator. It is not a water park to which I have paid admission. Though I was born in the coastal plain of North Carolina, my mother moved us back to upstate South Carolina after my father's death in 1959; with the exceptions of a year out west, three in Virginia, and two in the mountains of North Carolina, I have lived my life in the drainage of the Pacolet River. Upon my father's death I was introduced to the rich flow of the Piedmont's declining mill culture where my mother's family had worked in cotton mills for two generations. My mother's family's personal history (which was mine as well) was hardscrabble and stained by long hours and low pay. After migrating from the mountains, they moved in tightening geographic circles from mill to mill, pursuing jobs, working shifts, and living in company-owned mill houses in villages sprawled over hillsides right next to the river and its tributaries, the Fairforest, Chinquapin, and Lawson's Fork Creek.

Now the mills have all closed down, and in many places the forest has returned. I can see from maps that the river's final thirty miles below where we paddle meander past four abandoned cotton mills—Converse, two mills at Clifton, and Pacolet—and on through miles of pine plantations, impressive stands of oak and poplar, and a few remaining farms. I do not pretend to know much more than the maps tell me about those lower stretches. The river, before it meets the Broad, keeps to itself and is hard to see from roads; I've never paddled it.

"Is 'Pacolet' an Indian word?" Betsy wants to know.

"Yes," I explain. "One of the theories as to the origin of the name 'Pacolet' is that it is a Cherokee word meaning 'running horse.' Others say the river was named for a French man who settled in the county early on. No one seems to know which is true," I add.

"Why aren't there more rapids?" Russell asks.

I tell him there were once three impressive river-wide waterfalls in the mile-long trough of steep, erosion-resistant rock known as Trough Shoals about fifteen miles below the stretch we are paddling. The first town there was even named Trough. The river, however, was dammed, and the steep drop of the river converted into power, enough to turn thousands of spindles. Later, when the town changed its name, the waterfalls were long forgotten beneath the waters of the impounded river. Russell, the lover of adrenaline, likes my story of the waterfalls. He asks if we can ever paddle them. I have to admit that there is something compelling about those waterfalls trapped beneath the waters backed up behind an inactive dam.

We stop and eat our lunch on a sharp bend where the physics of the river has created a sandbar on the inside curve. As the water sweeps downstream, the heavier sand held in suspension by the current drops out first as the river is pushed toward the outside of the curve. A few miles upstream from this spot was once a bend so wide and a sandbar so thick that locals called it "Cowpens beach" until an enterprising sand and gravel company bought the site and mined it out for concrete production.

We eat our sandwiches in the sun on the small beach. All around the kayaks black freshwater mussel shells lie open like angel wings on the sand. I comment on their beauty, but Betsy reminds me that they are a sign of how compromised the river really is. They are an intrusive Asian species that has driven out the native mussels.

After lunch we return to our kayaks, pack the trash into the empty dry bag, and head downstream. A few minutes later I realize we've floated along as quietly as a raft of ducks. Even Russell sees the beauty of such a gradient-free float so close to town. He seems reflective at moments, a rarity for a rambunctious ten-year-old. He has settled into the pace of our outing. Then suddenly he's singing at the top of his lungs. We pass the heavily wooded banks and they retreat behind us. As if in answer, a dusty blue kingfisher taunts the river from limb-to-limb with its shrill, cackling voice. The river offers a child's joy for unconstrained spaces where Russell can push the boundaries of what's acceptable in polite company, and he fills it with his whoops. It's only when Russell's vocalizations are answered by men on a high bluff above the river that some of the joy goes out of our journey. It looks (and sounds, with sporadic hammering filling the air) as if they are building a deer stand, though it is hard to tell, looking up through the woods. "You better duck," the men yell in accents as shrill and local as the kingfisher. "We might start shooting." Betsy quiets Russell, ushers him between us. We float on in silence with only the sound of the men's hammers following us downstream.

Soon after the hint of trouble, the Saturday river turns turbid and deepens. For a mile or more we paddle across the mill pond I know is backed up behind the dam at Converse. Around one bend two men are fishing in a bass boat, and someone has cleared a pasture down to the water and built a small dock. A Muscovy duck paddles along the muddy river edge. Russell's earlier screams of freedom now come out as moans of outrage at having to expend energy to move his boat. "Around the next bend," I keep telling him, not really knowing for sure when or where the dam will appear.

We pass a big bend in the river full of dredging equipment where a local concrete company has been mining sand for decades. In its weekend idleness the dredge looks like some rusted industrial dinosaur. "Someone has gotten rich mining the river for sand," I explain to Betsy as we float past the spot. I find this ironic, how over the last half century many of the concrete buildings downtown have been molded from the river bottom itself. We drink its water, share its power, mine its sand. The river gives in all ways and ceaselessly.

I finally spot the mill. I have somehow paddled a few hundred yards ahead of Betsy and Russell. I turn my boat and look back upstream and can see them working toward me over the surface of the impounded river. I float a few moments without paddling, sit still on the surface of the pond. I can hear the falling water of the mill dam only a few hundred yards in the distance. The river forms a horizon line as it plunges in a perfect fall over the rock dam. Just downstream from every Pacolet River mill (Fingerville, the Clifton mills, Pacolet) there is a dam such as this one, which at one point may have produced electricity to power the manufacturing processes before the advent of the power grid.

The Piedmont cotton mills always had "a village," a company-constructed community, a clutch of wooden houses, now often sided with vinyl and altered by ownership. And of course, there is the river itself, channel and flow, which for years swept away effluvium of diverse origin: sewage, process dyes, dead dogs and cows, garbage of settlement. There is a tough species, the catfish, still living in the impaired waters of the postindustrial stream. Now that the mills have almost all closed, one is more likely to see these fish pulled from the deep eddies below the dams. If a Piedmont river has a soul, it is probably hidden in the swim bladders of these native bottom feeders. Their genetic predisposition is toward making the best out of the current's changing conditions. They are well suited to life in the Piedmont.

There is beauty in such a cultural landscape for sure, but for a moment I find this a scene of unaccountable hardship and suffer through the darkest nostalgia when I see the bricked-up windows of the old mill. I get a vague ache—the way amputees have described the nerve memory of lost limbs—when I consider these Piedmont mills and their neighboring rivers. My family tree is like one of the surviving river birches along an up-country stream like this one, the roots undercut by the eroding flow of our particular regional economic history (king cotton, king textiles, king development), the skinny limbs leaning out over the current, working hard for a place in the sun.

One element of this river's history I return to as I sit waiting for Betsy and Russell to catch up is the flood that roared from the mountains June 6, 1903. Historic accounts describe how a gentle rain fell for almost five days and then a cloudburst pushed the Pacolet to alarming levels. It was the single greatest catastrophe to ever befall the county. That morning, the slow music of the shoals turned into the cacophony of disaster. The waters swept away bridges, roads, and houses, leaving the small mill communities isolated from each other. Fifty people died, and three cotton mills were carried downstream by the power of the waters.

My Uncle Tommy's family worked in this same Converse mill "long as the mill had been open," as my mother says. Uncle Tommy worked there from 1942 to 1979, when it closed. His father had been the paymaster for the Clifton mills; his grandfather, born on April 13, 1903, a few months before the flood, was later the RFD mail carrier for that corner of the county. Once while visiting, I asked Uncle Tommy if he grew up hearing stories of the flood. "Didn't nobody talk about it very much," he said. The memory was deep and painful. People moved away because of the damage, and almost every family in the village was affected by the death toll.

What had he been told happened to his father and grandfather? He said that the mill whistle blew that morning to warn everyone, but most thought it was simply a call for work. "When the flood came, my Grandpa hollered for my aunt Helen and picked up my father Thomas. They came out of the house in knee-deep water." He waded with one child under each arm for higher ground, watching as the house was washed downstream.

"You can comprehend a piece of river," says John Graves, talking of the Brazos in *Goodbye to a River*. "A whole river that is really a river is much to comprehend." He says all a human being comprehends if he spends his life navigating a really big river—like the Mississippi or the Danube—is its "channels, topography, and perhaps the honky-tonks in the river towns." There are no river honky-tonks on the Pacolet. This is the Bible Belt, and besides, the river was never plied by riverboats, and barge traffic in the nineteenth century was very local, stifled by those shoals, those rocky ribs of gneiss.

I love rivers because they are real and not only metaphorical. In upstate South Carolina many of the very real rivers (we have always been a place defined by swift flowing water) were used first for power in the late nineteenth century by the growing textile industry; later, when power became more available, our rivers continued to be used as discharge channels for waste, human and industrial. I write about rivers because the ones I know best—those of the Carolinas—give me hope for the recovery of the land after great abuse. Even in the face of such abuse, a red clay river like the Pacolet endures, and our relationships with it endure.

Betsy and Russell paddle up behind me. Russell releases one final whoop of arrival as our friend appears with his pickup, which will carry us back to our car. We pull the boats ashore safely upstream of the dam and step out on dry land. I drag my boat through brush willows, yellowing sumac, and saplings of volunteer hardwoods, poplar and birch.

I am not tied to the Pacolet the way my uncle, mother, and grandmother were, but I still drink its treated water. I know that if it rains tonight the run-off from my city street will quickly find its way to a culvert and into the nearest "branch" and on down to the river in a day or two. Within two weeks that same water could be in the Atlantic Ocean. If the rain soaks in as groundwater, it might take years before it flows into the nearest stream.

I do not watch the river stained by red clay to gauge its flow, to dream its flood, or to fish it for extra protein, but I float it to gain some time to reflect, to recreate. I do not really know the Pacolet, but my history is adrift on it as surely as today I have drifted on the surface of this living stream.

Acknowledgments

These essays have appeared in slightly different forms in the following periodicals and anthologies:

"Confluence: Pacolet River," *Heart of a Nation: Writers and Photographers Celebrate the American Landscape* (Washington, D.C.: National Geographic Books, 2000); copyright © 1999 by the National Geographic Society. Used by permission of the National Geographic Society.

"Death by Water," *Terra Nova* (M.I.T. Press).

"Huxley," *Quarter after Eight* (Ohio University).

"The Ice Storm," *Creative Loafing* (Greenville, S.C.).

"The Inheritance of Autumn," *A Year in Place*, edited by Bret Lott and Scott Olsen (Salt Lake City: University of Utah Press, 2001). Copyright 2001 by the University of Utah Press. Reprinted with permission.

"Medicine Wheel," *Fourth Genre* (Michigan State University Press).

"Natural Edges," *State Magazine* (Columbia, S.C.); also in *In Short: Brief Creative Nonfiction*, edited by Judith Kitchen and Mary Paumier Jones (New York: W. W. Norton, 1996).

"The Once-Again Wilderness," *Ace Weekly* (Lexington, Ky.).

"One Family Line," *Southern Review* (Louisiana State University).

"Slurry," *Kestrel* (Fairmont State College, Fairmont, West Virginia).

"Something Rare as a Dwarf-Flowered Heartleaf," *Orion Afield* (187 Main Street, Great Barrington, Mass. 01230, 888-909-6568, www.oriononline.org, $30/year for 8 issues; 4 each of *Orion* and *Orion Afield*).

"Walking Kelsey Creek," *Hub City Anthology* (Spartanburg, S.C.: Hub City Writers Project, 1995).